DEMENTIA AND OUR LOVE

Caregiving as spiritual practice

ALSO, BY HEATHER FERRIS

Psoriasis, Healing from the Inside Out

Mindfulness, Awakening to a Meaningful Life

Someone I Love Died, A book to help young people deal with death

A story about children and loss

Please visit www.heatherjferris.com

DEMENTIA AND OUR LOVE

Caregiving As Spiritual Practice

A Memoir

Heather Ferris

Platypus Publishing

Copyright Heather Ferris 2024, © All rights reserved.

No part of this book may be reproduced in any form or by any means electronic or mechanical, including photocopying, recording, or by any other information storage and retrieval system or technologies now known or later developed, without permission in writing from the author or her delegates.

Edited by Jenny Ferris

Cover design by Infinity/Book Publishers

Book setup by Infinity/Book Publishers

Library of Congress Cataloging-in-Publication Data 2024

Ferris, Heather.

Dementia And Our Love, a memoir

Paperback   ISBN: 978-1-961617-88-9

Hardcover   ISBN: 978-1-961617-89-6

eBook   ISBN: 978-1-961617-90-2

Audio book ISBN: 978-1-961617-91-9

Health and Wellbeing, Self-help, Spiritual, non-fiction, relationships/personal development

1. Dementia 2. Caregiving 3. Relationship 4. Love 5. Compassion 6. Cognitive impairment 7. Mindfulness

Dedicated to Gary Greenstein, my beloved.

Thank you for your beautiful presence in my life and our commitment to loving during difficult times. Your poetry and words are indeed a gift. Thank you for willingly allowing this story to be told. May it be of benefit.

"We will always remember us this way."

Contents

Foreword	i
Introduction	iii
1 Who Are We?	1
2 Our Meeting	7
3 Intuition	11
4 Long-Distance Relationship	15
5 Risking Love	21
6 Aligning Our Life Values	29
7 So Many Memories From Southern Africa	33
8 Activism And Self-Responsibility	45
9 Memories Of Our Spiritual Path Together	51
10 Life In Canada With Dementia	57
11 A Heartfelt Approach To Caregiving	63
12 Grief – So Many Losses	69
13 Caregiving As Spiritual Growth	75
14 Gratitude And Learning	87
Acknowledgements And Gratitude	95
References	97
Further Information	99
About The Author	101

Foreword

As an Occupational Therapist and dementia care educator with over forty years of experience, I understand the importance of strong interpersonal connections, especially during the dementia journey. When the mind and body begin to change, the spirit remains. This enduring spirit and the relationship between individuals guide us through immensely challenging times, and it is what also yields brilliant moments of joy.

This captivating memoir explores the lives of two creative, spiritual, passionate individuals who found their way to one another. The included photos are spectacular and truly capture the essence of their lived experiences. The story then shares their walk through dementia together, hand in hand. I applaud Heather's commitment to developing her skills to be able to support Gary as well as possible, and for the courage to know when further assistance was needed.

Dementia and our Love provides a beautiful glimpse into Heather and Gary's life experiences and relationship. When two individuals are as deeply and spiritually connected as Heather and Gary, it is indeed remarkable. Their energetic connection is so powerful and exceptional that one cannot help but be touched.

Teepa Snow, MS, OTR/L, FAOTA

Founder, Positive Approach to Care®

Introduction

I turned my head and looked back out of the bus window in La Penita, Mexico, a tear silently trickling down my cheek. Gary stood smiling on the side of the road, waving his hand as the driver began our journey. I replayed his words, "Go with God," and me whispering, "Love you." Was this goodbye, or would we carry this newfound love with us and meet again? I needed to focus on my university studies back in Victoria, Canada. It required dedication to complete all requirements. I could feel the excitement of the past nine days, his tenderness, and how much we had in common. The bus increased speed, and my image of Gary became smaller each moment.

Is it possible that his journey into advanced dementia almost twenty-six years later is very similar as I watch him disappear into not knowing me as his beloved? The love is still strong, but the day-to-day management, dressing him, cooking, cleaning, organizing, and dealing with medical appointments took precedence. I was exhausted, not getting enough sleep, and had very little respite.

An interesting question that we generally don't contemplate when we fall in love: Is the love we experience with this chosen partner sufficient should they get dementia or another debilitating disease or situation? Ours was a later coming together in which love had to encompass the physical, emotional, and spiritual dimensions for both of us.

Are you a caregiver to a partner with Dementia, Alzheimer's, chronic diseases, and/or cancer? You will understand. I am the bearer of good news; caregiving can be an act of love that gives back to us. If we allow ourselves to truly grieve, we open ourselves to deeper love and joy. Love needs our attention, and it will sustain us even in times of fatigue, grief, and confusion if our awareness includes self-compassion.

Many of us are gallantly accompanying our loved ones through very difficult times. Gary and I were almost four years navigating dementia together. He was at home confused, not able to communicate, and at times not sure who I was. I sometimes responded with frustration and a lack of patience to his anger and resistance to my need for his cooperation. He was trying to convince himself and others that he was capable. I have, in my fatigue, sometimes not appreciated this dear man and how his disease was affecting our lives. I would go into helping mode and forget my heart, which felt like such a betrayal of our love.

Music has been a lifesaver. We regularly listened to bands on You Tube, both of us enjoying memories of the sixties and seventies and feeling aligned with one another. Suddenly, one day, Lady Gaga appeared on the screen singing, *Always remember us this way*. I was immediately transported back to Gary's and my love and to the incredible love story that is ours. It came to me that it would only die if we let it.

I knew the way forward: I could not let dementia's management take me away from my loving memories of our life together. Gary looked across at me with a smile and seemed to know what I was thinking. I know my eyes were sparkling, and my heart was filled with love and hope.

I remembered specific times and events: Mexico and our synchronous meeting, our simple marriage ceremony in Victoria, BC, that set the tone for our life together, long bus rides deep in conversation, or making love with such appreciation for one another. At this point, my heart was warming up. I shared an example of our love with Gary. His eyes softened, and we seemed deeply connected. He may not have remembered the event, but he felt the love. I wanted to remember us this way, and I felt re-energized. I played Lady Gaga's song many times.

Love is not just a concept but a felt sense, really remembering our values, what we did together, the reasons we chose to spend twenty-six years consciously loving one another. He was still unable to dress himself and unsure who was helping him. I felt tired, but my heart was different. I had more stamina.

I pulled out some sheets of paper one day and invited Gary to reminisce with me. It wasn't easy, but he did, at that time, remember some moments when I described them. I took notes and filled many pages, remembering more all the time. We laughed, his eyes were bright, and I became in awe of the life we lived and the people we were because of one another. I looked at him with a full heart, loving that we had chosen one another. He reached out to me to connect. This provided a respite from my tiredness, as I was getting something back for a moment. We became 'we' again rather than me feeling like an exhausted caregiver.

The ongoing dementia journey took many of the moments Gary and I had left together. There was little coherent conversation because of severe cognitive decline. I would recognize my fatigue, take a breath, and start with just one memory in the early days, reminding him of a time when we were together having an adventure in India or Africa, or just living our life. I noticed his eyes light up, maybe in response to my enthusiasm and my moving lovingly towards him. I said, "Gary, we have had a beautiful life together. Let's remember us this way."

We could do this dementia journey with love if we were able to do it together. It may be that opening our hearts to love in caregiving offers the potential for healing in ways not yet imagined.

I asked Gary if I could write about us and share his poetry and emails. He happily gave his permission. May it be of some small benefit.

1
WHO ARE WE?

Gary Lewis Greenstein was born in New York in June 1946, son of Jewish parents, Edward, and Rose Greenstein, originally from Poland a couple of generations back. He achieved a degree in mathematics from Cornell university, where George McTurnan Kahin and John W. Lewis in 1967 published, The United States in Vietnam. His professors revealed their writing to students, and Gary and others immediately became avid anti-Vietnam war protestors committed to peace. He saw the futility of materialism and was committed to resisting fighting in the war.

He left for Canada to get away from the USA, and at the border, he was told by officials that his father had died suddenly. Gary spoke of his dad as very loving, never judging his decisions. He was heartbroken and returned traumatized to New York and his family, anti-everything capitalist, particularly war. His father fought in the South Pacific during the Second World War and had been traumatized. Gary's heroes were anti-Vietnam war leaders and musicians and poets like Bob Dylan, The Band, Grateful Dead, and many other groups from that time. He lived for a while in Far Rockaway with his sister and mom as they grieved. He had some respite from the government regarding enlisting in the army. Gary traveled through Europe, spending time on a Kibutz in Israel valuing community living. He traveled on to Northern India through Afghanistan, settling there for a few months with many pilgrims involved in expanding their minds before returning home.

Dementia And Our Love

He was a poet. He said, "In Kabul, Afghani boys, obviously poor, came to sit with me in a park. They spoke no English, but they touched my heart."

Afghani Boys

Gentle brown eyes and silliness

Soft talk by whatever means,

To share the glow they give me,

The silent innocence

And love not yet scarred.

They learn stillness from the tree,

And peace from the mountain.

I wonder

Just how hungry they are,

But know,

How full of spirit.

Gary went on a meditation retreat at the Lama Foundation community in New Mexico, where Buddhism found him in the mid-seventies. He took the precepts to be honest, not to eat meat, take intoxicants or do harm. He worked as a tutor and bookkeeper/financial manager, volunteering with refugees, and spending his spare time meditating, including periods of six weeks at a time in silence with teachers Jack Kornfield, Joseph Goldstein, and Sharon Saltzberg, well-known these days.

He had relationships but often traveled alone, generally looking to contribute and be of benefit. He spoke most fondly of his work in Colorado with refugees from Bosnia, previously part of Yugoslavia. Later, while living in Canada, he worked with Syrian refugees. He loved skiing in the back country of the Rocky Mountains in Colorado. He considered Tuscan, Arizona, home in many ways. In 1997 he headed south from Tucson alone on a quest to Chiappas in Mexico. His family didn't understand his deep need to serve.

I am Heather Jeanne Ferris, born in the Eastern Cape in apartheid South Africa in 1946, the second-born daughter of Charles Ferris (from Scotland) and Inez Ferris, a fourth-generation, white South African originally from Europe. I have three sisters and a brother now living in South Africa, USA, Canada, and England respectively. My children are Kirstie, Wendy, and Robyn. I have five grandchildren.

My father, Charles, was a generous-hearted man with great respect for his children, four girls and a boy. He was a successful mechanical engineer in Johannesburg, South Africa, and at the same time, a sensitive/psychic/visionary who picked up on illnesses in people. My mother, Inez, was young and bright, a searcher of truth who encouraged my dad to follow his unusual talent. They raised us with the help of the book, *The Prophet,* by Khalil Gibran, 1926. "Your children are not your children; they are the sons and daughters of Life's longing for itself. They come through you but not from you, and though they are with you, yet they belong not to you."

They gave up a life of security and chose an extraordinary life led by their spiritual experiences. Meditation was a nightly ritual during which they connected with their own knowing. This resulted in their taking a fifteen-month family journey in 1953 to Lebanon, the birthplace of Gibran, and later England once the political climate demanded repatriation. They carried no funds to test faith and the power of God/Love. I was seven years old and the second oldest of their five kids.

I resonated with the retelling of the story of this journey, known to us as the faith trip, taking comfort in a simple life and, like my dad, was drawn into healing work and teaching. I was vigorously opposed to racism and oppression. My husband Stuart died in 1973 at twenty-nine years of age. I was his caregiver. After this, had someone invited me to an anti-apartheid meeting (they were all underground), I believe my life would have been the struggle against apartheid.

In 1975, I was a teacher of ten-year-old white children in Kensington, Johannesburg, pregnant with my first child. Macmillan South Africa asked me to write textbooks for Black children. I started my limited activism, becoming friends illegally with a principal and teachers in a Black school in Thokoza. The reality of apartheid almost broke my heart. I told Macmillan to get local Black people or someone in exile to write appropriate books for South African children. I was sad when the publisher said, "You realize, Heather, someone from Oxford, England will write them." I was not willing to collude.

I had married Bob, and with our daughter Kirstie, we left South Africa in 1976, as all but one of my family members had, and raised our three children in Canada, also living and studying in Australia and the USA. The marriage ended in 1989.

I resigned from my job as a school counselor in Qualicum Beach on Vancouver Island in British Columbia when Robyn, my youngest daughter, graduated high school in 1997. I registered for a master's degree in counseling psychology, took Buddhist precepts and planned to return to South Africa to volunteer during the HIV and AIDs pandemic. My grief at being separated from all people during apartheid was ever present in my heart.

School in Victoria, British Columbia, was intense but going well for me. My plan was to finish in one year. I would allow nothing to stop me, as I had waited so long to be able to go home to South Africa. Leaving there had been necessary but traumatic.

Gary and I were fifty-one years old, unknown to one another and happily single in 1997 when we individually headed to Mexico drawn by some force greater than ourselves.

I had driven north to Qualicum Beach, where I had raised my children, for a quick weekend. My good friend Kristeen flashed some airline tickets in front of my face. "We are going to Mexico for a month in early December, why don't you come?" I was about to say, "No way," but what came out of my mouth was, "Get me a ticket." She did.

I focused on school sixteen hours a day, seven days a week until December. I packed a small bag and met Kristeen, Roland, and their daughter, Lilyann, at Victoria airport. This was really happening, and I was feeling excited but crazy. How could I possibly be doing this?

Dementia And Our Love

2
Our Meeting

The plane landed in Puerto Vallarta, and we wandered out into the sunshine with no fixed plans other than to eat Mexican food, walk the beaches, and swim as much as possible. Our friend Jim had given us the number of his friend saying, "Joe will get you a good place to stay." The only instructions were to find him at Paradisio campground somewhere north of Puerto Vallarta. We climbed on a bus open to adventure.

It was hot and dusty when we got off the bus with backpacks and water bottles. We had no clue where to go but headed west to a beach, asking directions in English and not really understanding their response in Spanish. We bought some lunch and collapsed on the sand. Roland was carrying their heavy vegetable and fruit juice-making machine, I discovered.

A bearded gringo came up to us, asking where we were from and where we were staying. Kristeen said, "We are looking for this guy." She showed him a piece of paper with a couple of names. He laughed and pointed, "Well, that would be me, Joe," he said with a grin. "So, my old friend Jim wants me to find you a place to stay. My car is over there." We looked at one another in wonder at the universe stepping in like this to help us. We decided to trust the process and piled into Joe's SUV.

He told us about the area, trying to get a sense of what we would need. He kept looking at me to say yes or no, as he went from pensione to hotel. I shook my head. "I know the place," he said suddenly; Maria's in La Penita. We arrived at a hurricane-affected cement building right on the beach. No-one other than Maria was around. I looked at the crumbling accommodation next to a stagnant river. The price was relatively low, and I said, "Yes, we will take two rooms for a month." What was happening? The others looked at me incredulously but said nothing. We left our bags and headed off to purchase cleaning supplies, vegetables, and fruit for our smoothie bar.

We settled into swimming every day, making juice with fresh vegetables or local mangoes and bananas. We explored the area. My body was enjoying the heat, and I lay on the beach, relaxed, letting go of my life in Victoria with all its school-related demands. I meditated each morning, swam way out to sea, and felt I was in the right place. My middle daughter Wendy sent a message to say she and a friend were coming to join us for a couple of days. It was nearing the end of December, with our vacation over on January 9.

New Year's Day 1998 was sunny and warm with a slight breeze, the sound of the waves soothing in the background. We were lying around on the beach chatting. Wendy had a book lying on her towel, *Peace is every Step*, written by Thich Nhat Hanh, a Vietnamese meditation teacher. Her friend, Jen, from Victoria, was traveling with her. We were listening as they spoke of their adventures. Oh, to be thirty years younger.

A bearded, curly-haired traveler wandered towards us. He introduced himself as Gary and asked if he could sit down. He carefully placed his towel next to mine, or as I later figured, close to the book by Thich Nhat Hanh. He pointed to the book. I am Buddhist", he said. "I know this book."

OUR MEETING

I learned later that he had been traveling by bus from Tucson, Arizona, along a familiar southern route into the heart of Mexico. He was enjoying being solitary, reading, meditating, and checking out the scenery, going with the flow, expecting a three or four-day trip. Mazatlan was known to him from a previous trip.

Gary realized he was bored at being alone, pouring over his map as he considered his next stop. La Penita caught his eye. He whispered, "I haven't been there before." Settling back, he slept a little, then became curious. "Maybe I will find some interesting travelers." He settled in for the night, his head resting on his jacket against the window of the bus.

The following morning at 8 am, the bus ground to a stop, dust billowing. The conductor called to passengers wanting La Penita. Gary gathered his belongings and stepped out of the bus, checking out the lay of the land. "This road seems to go directly to the sea," he thought as he walked, red bag in hand, towards Maria's Hotel and his destiny.

The following few days, we walked the beach together. It was refreshing to have so much in common. It was a relief to talk about life this way. I didn't know anyone quite like him. We visited Playa de los Besos, the beach of kisses, with our group. It seemed significant.

January 5, Kristeen asked me about Gary as she and Lilyann had been talking. They saw us holding hands at the end of the beach near the graveyard. They must have missed our kiss. I am a strong swimmer. I had left Gary to walk back while I swam beyond the breakers back to Maria's.

January 7, Roland returned home to Canada. Gary, Kristeen, Lilyann, and I were constant companions. We got a ride to Chakala, a beach up the coast. Gary and I sat in the back of the truck, Kristeen and Lilyann in the front with the driver. Was that Gary's hand brushing against my leg, I wondered? Oh dear, what to do? My hand touched his. I could feel a stirring of excitement. We arrived at the beach in Chakala. Swimming was great. We both loved body surfing. We had fun together.

January 8, what a restless night, knowing that we were returning to Canada the next day. Oh, what I would give to snuggle next to him. I resisted. Instead, I headed to the beach in the morning to meditate, watching my desirous mind as the sun rose behind the town. The warmth of the sun saturated my back, bringing me deep peace. I felt his lips on my warm skin. I felt sad. This was about to end.

Gary hurried off to do an important errand in town while we packed our bags. He bought friendship bracelets for each of us. He placed mine around my wrist. I knew I would never take it off. I felt fourteen. We said goodbye at the bus. I whispered, "Love you". He said, "Go with God." The bus took off. I felt a tear roll down my cheek. Another breath and La Penita was gone. Gary stayed on at Maria's.

3
INTUITION

As I traveled, I reflected on this unexpected whirlwind of intrigue in Mexico and what I needed to complete at home to stay in this magical flow. My choice of topic for my major project was intuition and its role in decision-making. Why had I chosen that now? I had attributed it to my dad and his work, but I had been consciously teaching about it for many years. There were so many instances where I had followed my intuition with results difficult to imagine.

In Australia, I was a workshop presenter and facilitator. In Canberra in 1986, I presented workshops at the Adult and Community Education conference, one being *Using Intuition in your Work.* I had a few stories to tell about synchronous events and many participants shared deeply about their experiences. It went well and seemed to provide what they needed. I felt in the right place doing this work and people were enthusiastic.

We socialized that evening; my sister Shirley was there as a presenter from South Africa. We so enjoyed being together, celebrating our sisterhood and our work. I found myself tearing up as I met with colleagues. What was this about? I felt vulnerable and paid close attention, feeling as though I was pulling away. I was leaving. Where was I going? I meditated to see what showed up, and the feeling persisted. This was not an emotional response; it was far deeper.

I knew this from other times in my life when something was unfolding. My marriage was not great, my work was creative. What would I say to Bob and the children when I arrived home?

I asked Bob if he would consider a move away from Australia, expecting a resounding no. Instead, he sounded curious and interested.

This allowed me to trust this urge. We discussed where we would go. I had loved California, but we had no green card. Canada had been so cold. We decided to sit with it.

The following day, a letter arrived from my mother telling me about Vancouver Island, where they lived. "It is amazing," she said. "The mountains are snow-covered in winter but beautiful for hiking in the summer. There are lakes and of course, the ocean." She had not heard about our moving possibility. She also spoke of the meditation groups and writing coming through my dad. I could feel my inner engine get ready for action.

Bob was keen to return to Canada. The kids were excited to visit with their grandparents. Our faith trip was now in full swing. We sold our house, packed up our belongings, bought one-way tickets and hoped we had not forfeited our right to enter the country. We headed off with no security, job prospects, housing, or friends. It felt right.

All went smoothly. We landed in Victoria, met by my ecstatic parents, and traveled to Qualicum Beach where they lived. It was a quaint town with a rocky beach and warm ocean in the summer. That was a surprise and we all spent wonderful warm days together swimming. It was time to look for work, and Kirstie declared, "You can go and find a job, but we are staying here with grandma and grandpa. We are tired of moving."

I imagined working there but couldn't imagine being a workshop leader, the population was very small. What would Bob and I do for a livelihood? He wasn't concerned. I registered the children in school and investigated jobs in the school district. There was a youth counseling position at an alternate school. I said yes. Their beginning of year field trip was winter camping in snow caves, brrrr!

We bought a house. A year later, another job came up as an area counselor in the school district. They encouraged me to give workshops, and I felt a sense of belonging and rightness. Bob moved to Victoria, and we parted ways. I participated with my parents in their work, and when Wise Decision-making was born, I helped to structure it as a teaching tool.

Buddhism entered my life four years later. I had another relationship that seemed to produce many esoteric experiences. I always felt that everything had a purpose. We had broken it off, and I was very confused. A call came in from my friend Shelah, who was a psychologist studying with me in Australia. She was on sabbatical and traveling in the Caribbean and wanted to catch up.

I told her the emotional mess I was in. She said, "I will give you three weeks." I had no idea what she was talking about. I shared my woes, and after listening deeply and hearing about them more than once, she said, "Heather, you have told me that before. What are you doing?"

"Shelah, you are not very compassionate," I said abashed.

She replied, "You don't realize just how compassionate I am. Do you want to get through this or not? I can always leave."

I was shocked but knew I needed what she had to offer. She shared Buddhist teachings on suffering, the causes of suffering and the cessation of suffering. Basically, stop incessant stories about what is causing you harm. Feel feelings as sensations; be patient and watch them dissipate. Everything is impermanent. This is life. She had me read teachings, and they resonated deeply.

Karma and ongoing causes and conditions take us where we need to be. They are not always evident, the path not clear, often littered with confusion and distress. There were many conditions that came together to create Gary's and my karma in meeting. Living in Qualicum Beach, Shelah introduced me to Buddhism, knowing Kristeen, who purchased the tickets to Mexico and encouraged me to go with them. Speaking with Jim, who insisted on us finding Joe (who we met by chance), who drove us to Maria's; Wendy arriving for a few days and bringing a Buddhist book to the beach; Gary traveling south not really knowing why (he later visited Chiapas and could not stay), randomly choosing La Penita and Maria's. It is a miracle that we met and fell in love. We are all experiencing this in various ways. It is like mycelia making underground connections bathed in awareness. Is this intuition?

DEMENTIA AND OUR LOVE

4
LONG-DISTANCE RELATIONSHIP

I needed to get ready for school and my commitments. There was no time to daydream about the curly-haired stranger, that was until I received his first email two days later. Poetry was his way of processing. Gary sent this:

My passion fills the air
Like the steam coming out of
The elote woman's pot.
I avert my eyes
From the almond-colored breasts
That the young women like to show off
Wearing low-cut, tight tops.
I wonder if the fisher boys
Spend their nights half awake,
Immersed in erotic dreams,
With only the sound of waves
To calm them until dawn.
You had to mention loving to swim naked,
Now I lose myself imagining us on tiptoes,
Our chins above the water

Dementia And Our Love

Our mouths melting,

Bodies pressing, begging to fuse,

Rocked by earth's rhythm,

All senses wide open,

You, wanting to be entered,

In more ways than you care to admit.

I was touched by the poem that deliciously punctuated my psychological texts and lectures. Back to work. Another poem had arrived.

Love's Magic (still in la Penita)

My heart rings out with joy

Like the bell at the little church

Beside the plaza

Calling the people to prayer.

I sit there now,

Hundreds of birds screeching

Remembering your hands.

Strong hands like those

Of small, brown-skinned women

Slapping out tortillas

To feed maybe too many children.

And I, the gringo gypsy,

I sat on the beach this afternoon,

Talking to you

Of the magnificent floating vulture

Gliding with such ease,

Wings translucent with sunlight,

That I could only respond

Long-Distance Relationship

With tears of gratitude,
A spirit guide showing me,
It's all this easy
If you trust what you know.
I want to make love with you,
Not with our sexual organs,
But breathing Ishq
Into each other's mouth.
You know Ishq, the love nectar of the gods,
The creator of sand and ocean,
The vulture, you, and me.
The moon rises near full,
And all I can do,
Is eat pescado under fluorescent lights,
And promise to search for the ibis,
And for patience.
So, what do the bells of my heart call out for?
Simply a home, and someone to grow old with,
And a good channel for my energy.
I guess I'll just have to ride
The whales north in the Spring.
I'll tell them you'll be sitting there,
In the early morning sun
To drop me off in your arms,
An unusual catch of the day,
Or maybe love's magic.

    University had changed from concentration and fulfilling obligations to possibility and magic. Anything could happen, as it had the previous October when I had put in a proposal for my major project.

I had decided to take my dad's rather esoteric work into my research. My topic focused on the use of intuition in decision-making, using The Wise Decision-making Process. My tenured professor wasn't too sure he understood what I was doing and asked me to give him details.

I quietly planned what I needed to do, no-one else knew. I thought of going back to Qualicum Beach, where I was known, to facilitate a workshop and ask for people to participate in my study, all before the end of October.

It was a stretch, and I had questioned my sanity. I sat down on my meditation cushion in my house to go through the process of wise decision-making, which required about thirty minutes. At the twenty-minute mark, I heard a disturbance outside and decided to investigate. It was the garbage truck. I went back into the house and heard the telephone ringing. I answered.

"Hello, is this Heather? I am Steve, the organizer of the professional development conference in Qualicum Beach. We would like you to provide a workshop for teachers and support staff on October 23."

I took a breath. "What topic?" I asked.

"Anything you like," Steve replied.

"Wise decision-making?" I asked.

"Sounds perfect," said Steve.

"Steve," I asked tentatively, "Do you think I could invite participation in my research?"

"I can't see a reason why not." He replied. "Will $900 be okay for the day?"

"Sure," I replied. "See you then."

I hung up, packed my bag for the day, almost out of breath. What just happened?

At the campus, I went to see my professor. I told him about my morning. "Whoa," he said, "You better do it." I was his last student that he supervised. His cancer came back, and he died shortly after my graduation.

The workshop was very well received, and six people had signed up to be part of my research. It was beginning to feel easy if I focused on my life and let go of trying to control the outcome. It was obvious that my meeting Gary in Mexico was part of the plan. My guidance was to let go and let God, as my father would say.

DEMENTIA AND OUR LOVE

5
RISKING LOVE

Gary and I spoke on the phone a few times. He sent loving emails:

> I realize why I cry after reading your messages and talking to you. In my previous three relationships of the past twelve years, despite what occurred on the outside, in the core of my being, I felt alone. So, my ego manifested in many ways, and I was not willing to surrender to the relationship. With you, I feel communion in the core of my being, and that changes everything.
>
> Buenos suenos,
>
> Gary

I wrote back long emails about my courses and growing awareness, my hospice practicum, and my new sense of being in love in each moment.

> Gary, Why do I bring you into the deep recesses of my mind? Somehow, I meet you there, and we don't have to hide. I want you to see me transparent and still love me. I want to see you transparent and know I will always love you. The feelings I feel for you are all encompassing and embracing. I know they are real when we speak and in the silences between our words. The fear comes when I let the daylight in and try to find reasons, where at present there are none that answer the how's and the why's. I am becoming as smooth as the rocks on the beach that are caressed by the water a zillion times a day, if I can lie still enough and not cast myself too high upon the beach. Do you understand my ramblings, or do I wander too far across the line of my imagining? I open myself to your love, that it may benefit all sentient beings.

Dementia And Our Love

>Muchos besos,
>
>Heather

Heather, I feel our relationship is about taking risks. That is true for me. I feel rather crazy right now, my body tingling most of the time, my mind resisting not being in my body. It's as if all of me is being realigned. I feel vulnerable telling you this, yet I am unable to withhold from you. I feel your love. I am blessed.

>Gary

>An important poem that has inspired my life:
>
>Only a Person who Risks is Free
>
>To laugh is to risk appearing the fool.
>
>To weep is to risk appearing sentimental.
>
>To reach for another is to risk involvement.
>
>To expose your ideas, your dreams,
>
>before a crowd is to risk their loss.
>
>To love is to risk not being loved in return.
>
>To live is to risk dying.
>
>To believe is to risk despair.

RISKING LOVE

To try is to risk failure.
But risks must be taken, because the
greatest hazard in life is to risk nothing.
The people who risk nothing, do nothing,
have nothing, are nothing.
They may avoid suffering and sorrow,
but they cannot learn, feel, change,
grow, love, live.
Chained by their attitudes they are slaves;
they have forfeited their freedom.
Only a person who risks is free.
– anonymous

I responded to his invitation to risk:
I want to know you and walk with you,
Without fear,
And yet I do fear.
I fear myself and my desires,
I fear judgment from my children,
I fear moving off my path,
I fear the good-byes.
I want to know the pain and insanity,
In both of us.
I want to learn that your pain
Is not my fault,
That I cannot save you, and
That I can hold you in love,

That we can heal.

I want to experience our love and

Commitment to life

And give grateful thanks,

That we have chosen this life together.

I give myself freely to life and to you,

To hold on behalf of life

Fuel for God's sacred fire.

Gary responded with words from Pema Chodron from her book *When Things Fall Apart*. The first chapter entitled, *Intimacy with Fear,* says, "It is not a terrible thing that we feel fear when faced with the unknown. It is a part of being alive, something we all share. We react against the possibility of loneliness, of death, of not having anything to hold on to. Fear is a natural reaction to moving closer to the truth."

This is applicable too when facing dementia and other palliative diseases. The author suggests we get to know fear, become familiar with it, look it right in the eye. This develops courage and humility and dissolves arrogance or thinking we know.

His email continued,

> When we were in Mexico, I had two flashes of intuition. One was that we would work together. The other was that I had something to give your daughters. I am curious why you think they will judge you. I feel closer to you after each email. It's as if I am reading what's in my heart, what no one has ever understood about me. I meditate and hear voices saying, "Surrender, just surrender to this relationship." And I know they are right because I have never been with a woman like you.
>
> Buenos suenos,
>
> Gary

I had decided that if my major project and research were finished by April, Gary could visit. Many synchronous happenings, as well as hard work, resulted in my presenting my work to my professor before anticipated. Spring break was fast approaching. I was moving towards my long-anticipated visit from Gary.

> So, you are coming to me in April. My heart is warm with anticipation, and my spirit sings. I stand under the elephant-trunked trees in Beacon Hill Park on my way to the ocean. I feel their majesty, and I feel small and insignificant. The things I give too much thought to dissipate and take their rightful place. The path takes me along a cliff, and I look down. The sea is full today, and it calls me to come and play. I feel drawn to the element that bore me. Love fills my being, and gratitude for being alive in this place pours from me. I remember Mexico, and I am there under the waves, being held by the mother, finding the silence and acceptance I so crave.
>
> Buenos suenos to you too.
>
> Heather

Gary decided to go on a meditation retreat in Tucson before leaving to come north. It was essential that our relationship be grounded in spiritual practice. I meditated daily. He then bought a Greyhound bus ticket to Victoria, British Columbia via Seattle and Port Angeles, Washington. He spent two nights on the bus, taking in the changing scenery during the day. He took his time so that his arrival would coincide with my Spring break in March 1998.

The ferry left Port Angeles at 8.30 am for Victoria, arrival time 10 am.

That day I was at the ferry dock early, excited, a bit nervous. I hadn't seen him in nearly three months; pink cherry blossoms were everywhere. I parked my station wagon called Goldie and strolled in the sunshine.

Fear rose. "I wonder if he will show up?" I saw people going through customs. "Where is he? Is it possible that this is really happening? Maybe we won't get along". I would have been ready to go home at any moment if he had stood me up. I saw a guy in an Avalanche baseball cap looking around as if he was expecting someone to meet him. "Can that really be Gary here on Canadian soil on this sunny day"? At that point, we both moved fast. I felt his arms around me, the love warm and real. Whew!

He expected to be staying in a guest room. I had made space for us to be together. He didn't complain. My house in James Bay was as far south in Canada as I could have chosen to live. Kirstie and Wendy, my two older daughters, lived there too, sporadically, as did my dog Sprocket.

After a few days becoming familiar with Victoria, the capital city of British Columbia, we traveled north to meet my parents and my daughter Robyn, and to reunite with Kristeen, Roland, and Lilyann. Then we headed to the west coast of Vancouver Island exploring mountains and forests for three weeks before my next course and his departure. We drove and talked, listened to music, camped, hiked, and loved. We attended the Buddhist center, and my teacher was happy.

Gary was enamored with the ancient trees. He loved the mountains and ocean. He came from the desert. Time passed quickly. We shared our beliefs, family values, and my dad's extraordinary experiences as if in a hurry to get on with our lives. Everything needed to be transparent.

He shared that my dad asked him why he doesn't let people see him. I felt he let me see him. I imagine knowing my dad was psychic was a big risk. I asked Gary if he was holding back, and I assured him I could handle any truth. He said he was a little nervous. He was in Canada, getting to know a big family (lots of women). He was in my community with my friends and family. I guess that could be nerve-wracking. The time of love and poetry was settling into some form of reality. We declared our love with a dedication to speaking the truth. We spoke of a future together.

I dropped him off at the Port Angeles ferry, confident that we would be together. The ferry moved towards the horizon, and my mind returned to my courses and commitments at the university.

I was more relaxed after his visit, so I could concentrate on all the final courses, papers, and my practicum. My focus was completing my degree and being present to Wendy, Kirstie, and Sprocket.

DEMENTIA AND OUR LOVE

6
ALIGNING OUR LIFE VALUES

We wrote and called regularly. The plan was to spend time on his turf in the United States for our next meeting in July, after my graduation. Our destination was the Lama Foundation, a spiritual community in New Mexico. Gary met me at the Greyhound bus station in Taos, New Mexico. What a long trip, three days, all the way from Vancouver. Gary and I chose to use the buses because of the cost and our commitment to climate change.

Gary's values regarding simplicity and climate change were deep. I wanted them too, but it was a stretch for me; very uncomfortable, and when traveling this way, it required patience and flexibility. I could see that this relationship was going to teach me to walk the talk. This was what our love and commitment to life were about.

Lama Foundation was very important to both of us. It is a community that values many different spiritual practices. They call it the meeting of the Ways: accepting everyone no matter what religion, ethnic group, sexual orientation, or racial demographic. Communication was key, and talking about feelings was essential. Physical work was part of our daily routine, helping wherever it was needed.

We learned natural building as the community is off the grid. Indigenous elders, on whose land we were, came and offered teachings and ceremony. Gary and I met in the meditation kiva with others at 6 am each morning, before the morning meeting and practice.

These routines became an essential part of our lives wherever we lived or traveled. We knew our love would thrive if we lived kindly with others and the earth and if meditation was a core practice. We saw one another in action, working, praying, living together, and became confident that we could make it as a couple. We spent a few months at Lama Foundation each year, sometimes separately, many times together. Many people did this, and it felt like we had a large extended family.

We returned to Victoria towards the end of August 1998 and decided to get married in September. I was a bit embarrassed having another wedding, but it was important for Gary's legitimacy in Canada. Furthermore, Gary and I wanted to commit for life so that we would work diligently with what came up in our power struggles. I agreed. It has proven correct. We have lived that commitment and continue to do so. Within this, we have had a spaciousness where truth is essential.

Once during the dementia journey, when I was away with Gary in respite, he had two falls. I was hurt at the thought of him being there without me, but I was exhausted and needed to renew my strength. This is the truth, not some romantic ideal. We committed ourselves to being truthful, agreeing that even in the middle of our wedding ceremony, if we had second thoughts, we could pull out.

Our Buddhist teacher performed our wedding ceremony witnessed by my parents and a few family members and friends. It was the full moon. We have celebrated and renewed our vows every full moon for the last twenty-five years, even during the beginning time of dementia, when Gary had cognition.

Gary's vows

I vow to practice the dharma (Buddhist teachings) as the foundation of our life together. I vow to take care of you in illness, old age, and grief I vow to express my distressing feelings to you without withholding I vow to speak to you gently and with patience I vow to support you in manifesting right-livelihood.

Heather's vows:

I vow to practice the dharma daily so that our life together will benefit all sentient beings I vow to love and care for you always and continue to practice patience and compassion I vow to deepen my capacity to listen to you and seek always to understand and learn I vow to live my passion and my truth and express that which is inside, be it fear, pain, doubt, joy, or laughter.

We saw this as a work in progress and had to deal with normal relationship difficulties, always speaking about what was happening between us. I asked him what he did when in conflict. He said, "I speak up no matter what and get it off my chest." I reflected that he sometimes spoke loudly with some anger. He didn't quite see it that way at first.

He asked me about my style in conflict. I said, "I go away and think about it and then express myself without causing harm." We considered typical nervous system responses: fight, flight, freeze and quickly realized he was a fighter, I was a fleer. We committed to call one another on this pattern. If he became forceful in his opinion and I felt bruised, I would say, "You have to say that differently without bruising me." He didn't believe me at first, but it helped us change.

If I headed out for a walk in the middle of a disagreement, he would say to me, "Are you running?" I began to stay in the moment and breathe. I realized I had done this in my life because I was scared and lacked confidence. I wanted to be liked. In this relationship, our old responses would be different, and both of us experienced healing. That is love. Have we consistently kept our vows? No, but it helps us stay on track and review our behavior and fix unskillful moments.

During the time of Gary's dementia, I still reviewed my vows and took a deep breath, and tried again. I promised patience, I was sometimes impatient. I recognized my tiredness and accepted it; I then renewed my courage to practice patience. Practice in the face of difficulty strengthens me spiritually. I recognized Gary was not able to keep his vows with his illness; I accepted that too. I needed to take responsibility for myself.

Gary and I decided we would try to organize our livelihood to be able to travel as well. It was a dream, and we were going for it. Being in love gave us courage. A trip to South Africa was our plan for December. He couldn't take a job in the first year because of immigration requirements, and I decided to make work contacts that I could follow up when we returned from South Africa. Our house would bring in rental income, and we traveled very simply.

7
SO MANY MEMORIES FROM SOUTHERN AFRICA

We flew to Cape Town, South Africa. I wanted to meet with people of color and learn their perspective on the new South Africa. Maybe I could contribute in some way. I was curious how Gary would take me to my country and meet my sister and other family members. Table Mountain rose to meet me as the plane positioned for landing, and I was filled with excitement and hope, even as tears of joy slid down my cheeks. The immigration officer said, "Welcome home," sweet words indeed.

On the drive with Shirley, my younger sister, we passed mile-upon-mile of informal housing. I had naively thought there would be better housing for all people almost five years after apartheid was over. I could feel how much processing I needed to do as I came to terms with the poverty still rampant amongst people with Brown and Black skin. White people's lives had not changed much. I realized Gary was a perfect companion. He thrived amongst those with very little. He was not opinionated but patient as I processed my grief. He was open to following my lead.

It was wonderful to be with Shirley and her husband. They lived part-way up the mountain, far from public transport, so we walked the forty-five minutes to the main road and the taxis and trains most days. Gary and I fondly remembered those rides in crammed taxi vans, probably sixteen passengers, and the trains riding alongside the people I had so sorely missed during apartheid's oppressive laws. We laughed a lot and chatted with families wherever we were. They would ask why we caught the train rather than driving a car.

We were invited to do physical work at a retreat center in Kleinmond, a small town about two hours from Cape Town. The center was set up for post-apartheid healing. Our job was to dig out big roots and make paths in the shade of gum trees. A Black man came to chat with us at the end of the first week. He had been watching us and said it was inspiring to see white people working together equally, man and woman, doing manual labor while people of color were in workshops together. Maybe this was our small contribution. Gary and I walked in the hills, swam in the ocean, and loved being together working and having fun.

The HIV and AIDs pandemic was tearing communities and families apart, with many deaths and no medication. I knew AIDs. I had worked in Canada, providing HIV education and support to patients, families, and communities. People were approaching me to get involved, and I realized I would be traveling each year to South Africa for a while. Gary was receptive but wanted to know what he would be doing. "Trust the process" was my mantra.

We needed to consolidate our living situation in Canada, as well as Gary's immigration requirements. We needed to line up work so that we wouldn't run out of money. Our house would remain with tenants, while we rented a bachelor suite, putting our belongings in storage. This would test our ability to live harmoniously together with very little. I started a charity with a group of women, realizing that some of the needs in communities in Southern Africa would be addressed with those funds.

Gary's accounting background gave him opportunities for work in Canada and many chances to volunteer these skills in South Africa and Zimbabwe during the fifteen trips back and forth. I would go alone, or we went together depending on our work in Canada. I spent between two to seven months in Southern Africa each year. My counseling and training experience was useful in these traumatic and confusing times of HIV and AIDs. Our ability to be in a loving relationship together and be apart at times was a testament to the strength of our love.

We have special memories surfing at Muizenberg in Cape Town, as well as remote beaches, getting to know locals. One day, as we were hitchhiking near Port St Johns in the Eastern Cape, an old apartheid-style armored vehicle picked us up with two Black policemen up front. We were in the back with no way out, and it brought up our sorrow for the cruelty of apartheid. They gladly let us out when we arrived at our destination, a testament to their ability to forgive.

The surf was very inviting, and we swam regularly until one day, we noticed a commotion twenty yards down the beach. We came out of the water exhilarated from riding waves, but tragically, a young man's life had been taken by a shark a few minutes before. Life is precious. Were we living it well?

Long bus rides meant beautiful scenery and a sense of community while traveling. We were all putting our lives in the hands of the driver. Our karma was linked. We were equal. This is love. Small, sleepy eyes peeking around the back of the seat in the morning, shy, smiling faces welcoming us to a new day. After a rest stop, the smell of fried chicken and hot coffee with passengers willingly sharing. We were both vegetarian at that time, so we shared fruit, cheese, and sandwiches.

In Khayelitsha in Cape Town, Gary helped build a Habitat for Humanity house, working as a low-level worker for the Black builders for a week. They loved training him and so appreciated his humility and kindness. I was part of the procession through the streets with the family and workers when the house was finished. There was music and singing, smiles of gratitude. It was a mutually rewarding experience. The owners provided fried chicken, mashed potatoes, and coleslaw, and we all ate together.

I was to work that trip in the north-eastern part of South Africa. I met with organizers and considered the extensive program they wanted me to develop to provide counseling for children in fourteen villages. The work would have been interesting, but I was told explicitly that they were training children to be soldiers for Christ. I wasn't the right person and let them know. What was I to do instead?

A picture of Archbishop Desmond Tutu arose in my mind. I had read somewhere that he was opening an AIDs orphanage in Masiphumelele in Cape Town. My intuition brightened my thinking, and I purchased a train ticket to Cape Town, traveling with four women from surrounding countries, a touching learning experience. I arrived the day before the event.

A large crowd had gathered. I knew no-one. The "Arch," as he was known, was his usual mischievous and joyful self, but this was also a time for wise leadership. People who tested positive for HIV were often shunned and chased out of communities.

He asked the crowd what they would do if Jesus was present amongst them. They smiled and sang in joy, welcoming the thought. The "Arch" went on, "Well, I am here to tell you, Jesus comes in many disguises, and one of them is AIDs!" There was silence and then slow clapping as they took to heart his meaning. Love must include everyone.

This gathering led to me being invited by the ward counselor to work in Masiphumelele with women for at least six months. She said, "We have prayed to God to have someone work with the women."

The community was ravaged by HIV and AIDs with very high unemployment. We only went where we were invited. One day, some men asked us to follow them through alley ways, and we arrived at an informal drinking place colloquially called a shebeen. I think they wanted to shock their buddies, as they knew we were speaking of the transmission of HIV, which most people thought was only sexually transmitted.

We sat casually on upturned white buckets, as did the men. It wasn't usual for women to join them, let alone a white woman. I was probably seen as entertainment until I asked them questions about the community and HIV. They were silent at first, and I asked them if I could tell them how it is transmitted. Some nodded, and some made comments about sex workers and homosexuals. There was little eye contact, but everyone was listening.

I acknowledged that it was partly true but that anyone could get the virus. I knew many people infected who were neither sex workers nor gay. I was aware that apartheid had white-washed the truth about many things and cast Brown and Black people as being dirty, ignorant, addicted, criminal, susceptible to disease and generally the problem; all totally untrue.

I told them many white people were also infected. They were shocked. Racism has done her work demeaning the lives of Black people. We asked, "Can you get it from kissing, hugging, touching, drinking or sharing food?" They shrugged, and some nodded. We assured them that we also had to learn about transmission and were willing to share what we now knew.

Gary had experience with the men's movement in the states in the seventies and the ignorance about HIV transmission, basically blaming gay men. He shared the facts of contaminated blood, vaginal and semen transfer, mucus transmission and mother-to-baby transfer through breast milk, emphasizing that it could be prevented. There was no medication at that point.

The men looked serious and concerned, some looked deeply into their beer glasses and drank. They had been through so much: apartheid, violence, dislocation from their communities, poverty, and now HIV and AIDs.

I involved the health workers in the community. They asked if we could work together as people didn't trust confidentiality in a small community. I welcomed this opportunity. I felt humbled and learned so much.

The ward counselor had asked me to help women. Seventeen women and I met daily to talk about life, self-confidence, health (particularly HIV), family, education, and work. I connected with a foundation that provided a stipend so they could pay for childcare and food. They committed to attend together for a month.

The plan was both personal growth for the women, as well as income-generating, plus developing a community project to benefit everyone. We met in a wooden structure just big enough to gather in groups to talk, listen and strategize. We exercised outside in the street. They liked the yoga class with my friend Rosemary.

Bicycles were donated for the women as they spoke of the long walks to go shopping and difficulty getting to the health clinic. Women had not learned to ride a bike before, and they felt exhilarated. Where I live, we take so much for granted.

As people became closer, they acted in solidarity to protect one another from violence and to encourage speaking out. Most were women who had grown up in South Africa.

One woman, Aurelia, was a refugee from Rwanda who had lived as the wife of a diplomat and was trained as a teacher. She had been through severe trauma, having had her husband and a daughter killed violently in front of the family during the genocide. They had escaped Rwanda, run through five countries at great risk, and made their way to South Africa so Peter, the youngest, could be treated for sickle-cell anemia.

The women spoke of their lives in Masiphumelele and their needs, then set out to do something to mitigate them. A child-care center was established called Love and Care Day Centre. Women took on entrepreneurial projects: selling cooked meat, selling paraffin, sewing bags and clothing. HIV was part of everyone's curriculum.

Gary was welcomed by the men who were building a library. He was known as bicycle man. We were both totally comfortable with this simple way of life, and we made lifelong friends. Now in the middle of dementia lethargy, if Aurelia calls from Masiphumelele, Gary's face lights up. She checks up on him regularly. Her son's father was killed in the Rwandan genocide, and Peter regards Gary as a father figure. We experienced tremendous love in Masiphumelele.

Another time in South Africa, we took a long bus trip to visit my dad's sister and family in Durban enroute to Slangspruit. A friend of mine, Carolyn, had returned to South Africa, as I had, and developed a partnership with a school in this township near Pietermaritzburg, close to Durban.

Gary and I lived in that community for a few months alongside child-headed households. We experienced life in a room outside (second door on the right), behind one of the houses. It was made of clay and beams, very basic. Chickens, goats, cows, and pigs of all sizes passed by or nibbled on something tasty. We shared a toilet with other renters and washed from a basin of water as there was no bathroom.

The children and elders in the community were touched that we wanted to spend time with them. Gary helped teachers with computers at the local school, and I tried to understand the lives of children parenting their siblings after their parents had died.

The elders enjoyed the support and further understanding of HIV and AIDs that had taken their children, leaving grandchildren to fend for themselves. There was so much grief, and we gathered to allow it safe passage in a nourishing way. My friend Carolyn was committed to providing educational support for the older girls, who were in the roles of mothers, unlikely to get training for themselves. Many of the children looked lost. Their grief needed attending, so they knew they were not alone.

We stayed connected to Slangspruit for many years and visited a few times. Our charity in Victoria helped build a library for the school. Some of the children have died through drug use, and the trauma of their lives too great. Many have education and training. Some have their own babies.

Grief support for children was a focus for my friend Nontobeko and me for many years. We traveled in rural and urban areas, providing training for facilitators to run grief groups for children and youth. My book, *Someone I Love Died,* was written in five local languages to support these children.

Another warm memory in that part of South Africa was when we were invited to the Valley of a Thousand Hills in Kwazulu-Natal to teach meditation. By then, we were both experienced meditation teachers. It was semi-tropical, big trees, beautiful hills, and monkeys everywhere. A mist would descend into the valley and shroud this beautiful place in mystery.

The Masiphumelele community has grown exponentially over the years, with many people from countries north of South Africa coming to Cape Town with the hope of jobs and money to send home. Love and Care Day Center, now twenty years since inception, is much in demand. Aurelia is still the principal with a staff of eight. She and I are in almost daily contact.

Dementia And Our Love

8
ACTIVISM AND SELF-RESPONSIBILITY

We both had great difficulty with decisions taken by politicians in our countries, Canada, the USA, and South Africa. Racism was a common enemy to both of us, so we actively stood up against discrimination and worked towards reconciliation. We opposed nuclear power and arms at Los Alamos. The natural environment is important to us, and we tried to be conscious of cause and effect. We used biodiesel for fifteen years using only reused vegetable oil. Our car smelled like McDonalds. Gary worked and volunteered for a few environmental organizations. We walked, used buses and trains, and yes, we flew once a year, feeling bad about the use of fossil fuel. Growing food has always been an important part of our lifestyle wherever we have lived. Our life felt congruent with our values.

In 2003, the Iraq war started, and Gary was devastated by the US involvement from the mid-nineties. He used poetry to pour out his heart:

Dementia And Our Love

America
Your shadow has arisen.
The faces of Iraqi women
Cradling the bodies of dead children,
Crying tears, yes real tears
So that you can drive three blocks
To the supermarket.
America
Look at your bloody hands,
In fact, your whole-body dripping blood.
See sixty million buffalo,
Slaughtered for sport,
A people's food and spirit destroyed,
For what?
And from that day on it has continued.
America

Can you hide another day,

Or will the oppressed finally arise,

And give you back,

The terrors they have felt and seen,

So that you may know your blindness.

America

The glass case is broken,

The mirror revealed.

Lama Foundation in New Mexico was the America that brought hope back to us. It was built on the peace trail. There is a spring, a peaceful meeting place for Indigenous tribes to rest as moving through the area. We participated in prayers and dances for universal peace and generally held values and took actions towards a more peaceful and sustainable future.

The original founders were wise beyond their years, and after fifty years, Lama Foundation is still bringing people together, offering young people a different way forward. There are no religions or philosophies pushed, just many traditions that can open our hearts and minds. My parents focused on prayer and meditation, encouraging us to use our spiritual gifts and trust our intuition. What a gift to have had these experiences and now to be able to trust Life.

Gary and I felt that community living and sharing resources was important as an antidote to materialism and a responsible use of resources. We were drawn to communities in the US, Canada, and Southern Africa to learn from their experiences and share ours. One such community was Kufunda in Zimbabwe. Gary had found their website on the internet, a place where environment, meditation and humanitarian issues came together.

We spent three months there living in rondavels, round yurt-like structures made from clay with grass roofs. The sky was jet black at night, brightened by millions of stars. Zimbabwe has longstanding political uncertainty, making people poor and incredibly resilient. I headed out into rural areas as I had done in South Africa, helping people deal with HIV and AIDs. Gary trained community members in bookkeeping. We both helped with vegetable-farming experiments.

Towards the end of the three months, Gary had flown to Johannesburg to help at a different center, I was leading a weeklong training with women. They had asked for healing methods to add to what they already used. On the first night, I headed back to my house for a rest while women made a fire outside to cook. It was dark, with the milky way vibrant in the sky above my head. I arrived back at the fire, where I could hear the laughter and chatter of women's voices.

They greeted me joyfully as I made my way around the fire. I wasn't looking at my feet, and in an instant, my foot struck a round log and began to roll. The motion propelled me forward, and I landed headfirst against a brick wall. I knew I was hurt as all body functions went into shock.

"Please sing," I said to the astonished woman. I focused on their extraordinary voices, the melody dancing through the air. I asked one woman, Anna, to hold my head, the palm of one hand across my forehead and the other palm cradling the occipital area at the back of my head. It felt like waves of love around the top of my head that bled down through my head, face, neck, back, all the way through my body. The initial pain had settled, and someone had mopped up the blood.

Activism and Self-Responsibility

There was a suggestion that I be taken to the hospital, but I said no as it felt too risky. Anna took my hand and escorted me to my hut, where I lay on my bed. Anna settled on the floor next to me. She was not going anywhere, she said, but would instead tell me stories until I fell asleep.

I slept through the night and awoke stiff but without pain. One look in the mirror reminded me of what had happened. I was touched by the healing and so grateful for the women. We continued the training for the next five days. On day five, one of the women said, "We haven't learned healing yet." I reminded her of Monday night. I described my experience, and they practiced in pairs. My dad would do a headhold when we were children and not feeling well. It brings balance and grounds us into the present moment.

The memories of the people, animals, incredible rocks, and vegetation are special to us. Nowadays, Gary remembers little of that time, but the music brings it back. Mbira and drums hold vibrations of this amazing land.

One year, we were invited to go to Costa Rica to check out a retreat center where we could offer meditation. Costa Rica did not invest in arms and instead at one point, had a ninety-five percent literacy rate. We loved the courage the leaders took to create a place of peace. Guns were frowned upon, and we observed an art exhibition where all the exhibits were made of pieces of artillery. Peace is important to us.

We felt that this might just be a holiday for us, resting, walking together, meditating and body surfing. Gary had learned Spanish, so he had lots of practice, and it was so beneficial to be understood by local people. We smile when we remember the parrots, sloths, monkeys, and such lush vegetation so close to a magical beach. We would dive into the ocean together, catch a wave and beam at one another as we felt the sand come up to meet us on the shore. We never did return to teach a retreat there.

One of my great disappointments when I had moved to Canada in response to apartheid was the knowledge that Canada had given the blueprint of apartheid to South Africa. I became aware that the treatment of Indigenous people was close to genocide. Much of my support as a counselor was with people deeply traumatized by residential schools. The government's intent in removing children from their homes and communities was to take the Indians out of the child, destroy the culture, including Indigenous languages.

Our livelihood has always been congruent with our values and our vows to one another.

We had settled in the Cowichan Valley in 2007, just as the North American Indigenous Games were being planned for this area. The local Quw'utsun elders needed three thousand volunteers for this large event and wanted us to be familiar with their traditional teachings. We learned to drum and sing together. We participated in the sweat lodge. It has been a path of the heart with many humbling experiences. Gary and I were together in this, making many new friends and learning about this precious culture.

Our life was supported financially by my psychotherapy practice, teaching for City University and Gary's accounting work. It was still possible to be in South Africa regularly for a few months at a time. We were also visiting Lama Foundation for a month or two each year up until 2017. Looking back, we risked a so-called normal life without the trappings of materialism and instead experienced and learned so much.

9
MEMORIES OF OUR SPIRITUAL PATH TOGETHER

Walking together in simplicity, we are connected to everything.

Every memory could be considered part of our spiritual life together. In Canada, for the past fourteen years, I have taught a five-day silent retreat each May on Salt Spring Island at KDOL center. Before dementia, Gary would teach meditation with me. These times, meditating and teaching together brought peace to us. Now, meditation is difficult for Gary, but talking about it can be familiar and he sometimes would lie on the bed while I meditated, and it calmed him. The view from KDOL on Salt Spring Island is vast, like the mind.

Dementia And Our Love

India called us in 2010. We wanted to visit with some of our Buddhist teachers and walk the path of the Buddha in Bodhgaya and Saranath. Buddhism has been important to both of us. That has never waned. For many years, we meditated early each morning together until we were doing different meditation practices on our own. We regularly attended retreats with our teacher, Lama Kunzang (Lama Rodney Devenish), at the Hermitage Center on Denman Island in British Columbia, now known as Nature Nurture Refuge.

Our relationship has always nurtured what we individually needed, as well as our collective needs. We reminded one another to be grateful, to serve others and to keep everyone in our hearts, even those for whom we have irritation. On this journey, we appreciated how old this tradition is, as we visited ancient temples and shrines and famous teachers, particularly in the Tibetan tradition.

In Bodhgaya, we chanted alongside nine thousand monks at the Monlam with HH Karmapa and visited Thrangu Rinpoche at another of his monasteries. The extraordinary chanting, again, the vibration that connects us to all-encompassing love. We also traveled north to Bir, thinking we might get a glimpse of the Dalai Lama in Dharamsala. We wandered through the countryside on foot mostly, just to get a feel for India. We went around a hill one time and saw about fifty hang-gliders in beautiful colors suspended in the sky, a contrast in this dusty, ancient landscape.

Gary and I walked many miles through the north Indian countryside, marveling at how people live on very little, with community celebrations and joy alongside their difficulties. A street wedding involved anyone who was passing by. The DJ had a battery on the back of his bicycle, which powered the music, enabling the guests to dance together. On the train a wedding party provided food for everyone on the coach. It was delicious, and we felt a sense of belonging.

We decided to include Nepal in our plans. As usual, service was an important consideration, and we found the Rokpa Kitchen, a street feeding program in Boudha, Nepal. Rokpa had been started by one of my teachers, Akong Rinpoche and Lea Wyler. They had a children's home, providing a safe place for many children who had previously been unhoused and literally lived on the sides of the streets.

We worked there daily for three months, chopping vegetables and serving soup, meeting Nepalese people who lived precariously with little chance of paid livelihood. It is humbling to do this work and a great way to grow love. We lived in a guest house attached to a monastery, so we had access to meditation and teachings.

We spent countless hours connecting with people on the street. For many, it was their home, while others survived with a family in a room. We visited a family of four: Meena, her two girls and their boy cousin. There were two beds, clothes were neatly stuffed in bags. A small stove was set up between the two beds, food was packed in a plastic tote. What a delicious meal we enjoyed prepared by our host. Gary and I were so touched by the love and generosity of people living very simply. This family became our friends, and on a subsequent visit, we heard that the father of eight-year-old Surav had come out of jail and taken him. They really missed their cousin. Meena was worried for him.

We enjoyed long walks in rural areas. The farming is done around the contour of the slopes, not wasting any space. In the distance rose the majestic, snow-covered Himalayan mountains. We formed a particular connection with the Namo Buddha monastery and the teacher, Ven. Thrangu Rinpoche also has a beautiful monastery in Richmond, BC. He passed away in June 2023. We were so fortunate to be in his presence hearing his compassionate teachings.

Gary has always supported the Seva Foundation. He is known even now in his care facility by his red Seva cap, worn diligently to show his support. Seva was started by Ram Dass in the US. They are also in Canada, saving people's sight around the world. The director asked if he would like to visit one of their eye camps and teaching hospitals on the border between Nepal and India. He immediately agreed. Gary traveled first to Boudhanath, also known as Boudha, near Kathmandu, to volunteer at a small monastery teaching English.

He reconnected with Meena and her family. She cooked him an amazing meal after he arrived at their room with a bag of rice and a bag of flour. He walked with the children who remembered him well from two years before. The owner of a restaurant we had frequented asked him where I was. He smiled and said to Gary, "I remember she always wanted more vegetables."

His trip to the border was harrowing, the roads crumbling, the drop-off intense. Gary is afraid of heights. The eye hospital was busy getting ready for the eye camps where eye tests were done as well as cataract surgery. He felt enriched in this environment of generosity and care, which is at the heart of the work of Seva Foundation. It encouraged us to give regular support, knowing people could see. The philosophy is two-fold. If children's sight is restored or problems are detected early, they have a chance to go to school and possibly get employment. If adults receive surgery to restore their sight, they are not a burden on their families.

I was working in Canada while he was away, but I felt connected by our common commitment to Seva. Gary returned with many stories, the diligence of the doctors, eye camp staff, and the friends and family members who brought patients for cataract and other surgeries. They also did eye checks for children as prevention. You could see long lines of people making their way to the camp, the sighted leading those with minimal or no sight walking for many days.

We are not separate, we depend on each other, not just family and friends, but all members of this universe. In poor communities, people rely on one another. If you have money or food, you share it. Ubuntu is a South African word meaning, I am because you are. In Buddhist terms, the teachings say we are interdependent. This requires me to examine the cause and effect of everything we do.

Everything changes or is impermanent. This brings me confidence that my anger is not a fixed state, neither is my grief or happiness. The moment is the only time that is real, and then it is gone. What I do in this moment counts, so if I am awake (not distracted or caught up in desire or aversion), I am more likely to do something positive. Of course, like everyone else, I am not awake some of the time. Meditation is a good practice of being awake in the moment.

Buddhism suggests we have multiple lives, so what I do in this life could create karma in this life or the next. This helps me to act with more integrity because it has consequences. Climate change provides some evidence for this. My dad's teachings in *Twelve Dimensions* by Charles Ferris also speak of multiple lives. They suggest that we are evolving our consciousness so we have opportunities to become clearer and wiser.

Religions and philosophies give us guidance. What we choose to believe is up to us. Guidance is not a fixed state. Religion should not provoke wars or division by judging right and wrong. We humans have developed dualistic thinking, something is right, or it is wrong. This seems more like the nature of the ego.

Gary and I valued similar beliefs and teachings, so when he began to decline cognitively, we were solid in our love for one another. Our health is impermanent. We had the good fortune to be healthy together for twenty-three years. I was sad but not scared. I knew things would continue to decline as there was no cure. Gary was certainly not happy about the possibility of dementia. We humans are attached to our lives. In Buddhism, the teachings suggest the more attached we are, the more we suffer.

In my dad's teachings, he talks about the ego, or spirit, and the soul. The ego is necessary to house the soul for this life, so it naturally grabs at life, not wanting to give up. Cause and effect are at play, so we suffer. Gary's determination to live is a testament to his belief in the preciousness of life. As a caregiver, I still want independence, so the more I am attached to this, the more I suffer.

DEMENTIA AND OUR LOVE

10
LIFE IN CANADA WITH DEMENTIA

Face life as impermanent, take one step at a time, we are not alone.

Gary has been part of a men's group in the Cowichan Valley for many years. The men listen to and support one another in a healthy way. They care about one another. One day in 2019, one of his friends told me he was concerned as he was noticing changes in Gary. It made sense to me. He had fallen off his bike and broken his hip, which was replaced within a few days. His body recovered quite quickly. After this, his memory became problematic, so I booked a test for him. He went along with it hesitantly.

I didn't want to acknowledge the possibility of a dementia diagnosis. The way I responded with my first husband, when the doctor told me he would die in three weeks and I was to tell him, I was scared but knew we needed to face it. I accompanied Gary to his appointment and started reading the literature. He was quite quickly diagnosed with dementia. My initial intrigue was in his inability to recognize spatial cues. Up, down, back, front, next to, top, and bottom were curiously absent, and it is surprising how often we use them. He would stand 'in the way,' having no ability to strategize how we could plan our moves to accommodate one another. Gary's dementia coincided with the beginning of the COVID-19 pandemic, so everyone was inside their homes taking stock of their health. I was working online.

We live in Duncan, which is close to amazing rivers and mountains, a great place to camp with grandchildren in the summers. We were home. This was where we had settled. We tried cohousing, sharing with a woman and her young son in a simple two-bedroom, one-and-a-half-bathroom house with a garden. This did not last long. In 2010 we moved into an apartment next to a community garden, spending hours working alongside one another, growing amazing vegetables. We still traveled each year and worked in Duncan, connecting with a community of like-minded people.

After Gary's diagnosis in 2019, we could continue to live here easily, as we were already living simply and could manage the ongoing changes in Gary's health. The food bank, located on the next street, was very much part of Gary's daily routine. He took a bag of vegetables each morning for soup-making in summer and winter for thirteen years. This continued for three years after his dementia diagnosis, as his walk became a shuffle, and he became more unsure of how to manage the elevator.

Doctors said he had deteriorated fast. He endlessly asked the same questions, perseverating about something that had been said. He was restless, walking here and then there, zipping the zipper on his jacket up and down many times a day. It is part of sundowning, it seems. The jackets were fast becoming 'zipper-less.' Instead of Bicycle man, he was becoming Zipper-man.

He described his life as being without someone special, as I moved out of the bedroom because I was not getting enough sleep. I would go into his bed sometimes in the morning. Gary felt the loss. He felt helpless in terms of helping me or others. This caused him sadness. He referred to his need to help as a core value.

My ability to visit family was impacted. I felt the loss of contact with grandchildren who grew up fast. We have wonderful memories camping together. Zoey and Milo attended a camp in the community garden in the summers. Wendy's family came from Edmonton, and we enjoyed a couple of family reunions. We have traveled to their homes at other times, but Gary could not manage the traveling anymore. Our three double beds in our apartment were occupied recently when family visited. My sister Jenny and her husband, Charles, live in our building. They provide a comforting family presence.

Gary's walking quickly became compromised. If he walked too much (100 yards at most), he would go into what I call involuntary walking. His legs continued to take steps, and he couldn't stop. This was dangerous, particularly at the curb prior to crossing a road. If I tried to stop him, his body would continue to propel forward, or his legs would collapse. I couldn't manage it without help. Sometimes, I had to prop him up against a wall until his body rested.

He was no longer able to safely navigate the walk to the food bank unaided, but the routine and the kindness with which he was welcomed were very dear to him. I would go out and pick vegetables, dress him up warmly, put his lanyard with his name and my contact around his neck, with his keys. He would head to the elevator and maybe get to the ground floor and out the front door. I would then stand at the fourth-floor window, watching his progress, as we can see the food bank on the next street in full view of our apartment.

I would notice him knock at the door, be welcomed and taken inside, and then his red SEVA cap would reappear. He was ready for the walk home, always carrying the empty bag ready for the next day. This was his last piece of independence, his job. For a long time, he had regularly hung out at the library, very close to our apartment. He loved to read and would get advice from the librarian, who very kindly helped him to find a book, until Gary realized it didn't make sense anymore.

His life became centered around our apartment, and I tried to accompany him on a short walk outside each day, which was difficult for him. The doctor said he seemed to have Lewy Body Dementia, but he doesn't have Parkinson's disease.

Home care workers came to shower Gary and spent almost three hours, three days a week, towards the end of his time at home. That made a huge difference, although a different worker would attend each time. It is important for caregivers to have some time away. I would generally go for a walk, the gym, or shop for food at that time.

I work from home online, counseling or facilitating groups, and I began writing again. This allowed me to feel I had a life of my own. Gary would open the door to my office, and I would redirect him. We acquired a TV, and although we never wanted one before, it kept Gary entertained for a while. He liked to read the text for hearing-impaired people to practice his reading, although it didn't appear that he had much understanding of it. He spoke fondly of his grandma teaching him to read. It was hard for him as he realized he could no longer read coherently.

Thursday morning was the men's group until he resided in care, and his dedicated friends would come to drive him. They attended dementia awareness training to help us, which touched my heart. This weekly excursion was vital for Gary, even if he sometimes used the time to complain about me. A special friend would come to take him out on a different day. They went to help carve and paint a large totem pole in the community, Gary felt he had a purpose. These friends, Jim and Gary, shared a special connection until Jim was diagnosed with aggressive cancer and died after three weeks. Gary, at this stage, was confused. We visited Jim in the hospital, but the friend he had known was becoming a hazy memory.

I booked Gary into respite for a week at a time four times in 2023, including two weeks over Christmas to be with my children and grandchildren. He said he liked the respite home, as they had lots of good things to eat whenever he wanted them. I have been touched by the kindness of our friends who visited him when I was away.

We were always very community-minded prior to Gary's dementia diagnosis, and I felt quite removed from the community while caregiving. Activism takes energy that I don't always have, so I interacted on facebook and other platforms. It was comforting to know what was going on in the outside world.

If you visited our apartment, you would see photos along the hallway, memories of family, Lama Foundation, Southern Africa, and Nepal. On the coffee table were more photos of long ago that Gary would pick up and ponder. They seemed to look more familiar to him than those of the last twenty-six years, yet not clearly knowable.

In our bedroom are pictures of him and me. He mostly knew we were together. We wore our wedding bands, and he noticed for a while we both had one but did not know our relationship at times. It no longer seemed important for me to help him get this straight. I still appreciated him as a life partner.

Our full moon vows persisted until dementia took hold, and we would revisit our vows, and then it became enough to recognize the moon in her fullness each month. She was still watching over us.

On one of our wedding anniversaries a few years before dementia, Gary handed me this:

What I like about you:

> Playfulness with me
>
> Affection towards me
>
> Sharing spiritual path
>
> Sharing similar material values and lifestyle
>
> Supportive to me financially
>
> Caring of those who need someone to care
>
> Caring about the environment
>
> Commitment to our marriage
>
> Listening to my distress and that of others
>
> Openness to passion in lovemaking

I sometimes wonder what he would say now, reflecting on this path together in hindsight through dementia. I was always touched by Gary's thoughtfulness and gratitude. We both kept our marriage vows because they were based on our beliefs and values. Even through dementia, Gary would thank me occasionally, although in the latter stages of being at home, he held me responsible for his lack of independence.

Long-term caring for people with dementia is exhausting. The disease demands so much from caregivers, and if I didn't get enough support or a chance to fill my cup, I was not the kind, caring person I wanted to be. I didn't beat myself up when impatient. I noted that it was time for self-care.

Some of the most difficult times for me occurred when I was not well and had no one at home to care for me. I had an operation on my liver, a one-day procedure under general anesthetic. Kirstie came up for the day to be with Gary and spent one night. I returned to caregiving duties the next day.

I was always the caregiver, the one he turned to, the one with the medical suggestions, the one who answered all the questions from healthcare people. As time progressed, I felt he needed me as a toddler who demands attention from his mother. "Look, mommy is on the phone, how can I get her attention!" His lack of empathy was apparent, and this was not the Gary I had known for so long, and it wasn't personal.

I realized, too, that his awareness of his senses had changed. Food was something to eat, texture curious but not a delicacy. His hearing became acute, regular household sounds almost overbearing. It took so much concentration just to survive.

11
A Heartfelt Approach To Caregiving

Be where you are, right in the middle of things, without hope or fear.

Our apartment rang with tunes played by bands from the sixties, seventies, and eighties. Both of us would get transported into our carefree past. We enjoyed the same music. Sometimes, we danced or sang along. I used the music from the Traveling Wilburys, *Handle with Care* and *End of the Line* to motivate housework when my girls were teenagers. It made me energetic, and I thought of my daughters with love.

We watched Woodstock, and Gary was transported way back. He was there walking miles, as there were so many cars parked along the route. One summer, we went to a local festival called Special Woodstock for people with developmental diversity. Local bands played their music, and people danced up a storm. Gary wandered over to the organizer and told them he was at the original Woodstock. He was heralded as a hero.

Playing music was a regular part of life for us. Gary had a couple of flutes, and we had a drum. He could no longer use them as he used to, but he could still manage a tune on his harmonica in time to Dylan. I played my accordion and keyboard, improvising as I felt fit. I discovered amazing shows on YouTube about the Beatles, Michael Jackson, and the making of USA-Africa Live Aid as well as others.

My writing has always been a great resource for me. I was writing about being born white in South Africa as dementia was raising its head, but as the disease progressed, I focused on our love story instead, as it reignited our love and opened my heart. At one point, I had enough of the broken zippers on his jackets and sweaters, including those I had laboriously fixed many times. I needed space from him until I came out of my overworked, hurt self. I wrote and could feel my mood change.

A very useful teaching from Buddhism is to be where you are, right in the middle of things, without being in hope or fear. I sat with my tiredness and mental frustrations. I could feel how tight my mind was and breathed into myself kindly. It wasn't about Gary at this point. It was me being with sensations and breath. It was like a rope unfurling from its stuckness. Gary would come in and ask a question, and I would clearly say I was taking time to write and dinner would be ready soon.

Sometimes, I used a mantra, a series of words that have a positive meaning, when I felt I was about to explode. I don't like swearing, and when tired, those words are ready to fly. The mantra I used most was *Om Mani Padme Hum*, which the Dalai Lama has said in English means, *On the path of life, with intention and wisdom, we can achieve the pure body, speech, and mind of a Buddha*. I just said it over and over with the intention of changing the direction I was going from potential harm to kindness.

I like the kind and heart-centered approach to dementia care shared by Hilde Seal, who focuses on the spirit of people with cognitive decline. Hilde shares quotes from Teepa Snow, who is a well-known dementia educator. Teepa developed the Positive Approach® methods, which are very practical strategies for interacting with people living with dementia. Teepa also developed the GEMS® States, which helps people understand the changing states of the brain and how to best interact with individuals in the various states.

I found the sundowning restlessness the most difficult as I was tired by the end of the day. I liked a suggestion I heard of putting a soft scarf or a man's tie in one hand of our person with dementia to help them stroke that with their other hand. We can support them by taking their hand with ours. Soothing is important. Gentle touch can help too. Rubbing Gary's feet or hands with cream worked well. He also enjoyed a chest or back rub as his skin would get quite dry. A gentle wrist-stroking could bring peace.

The headhold I used in Zimbabwe is helpful. The palm of one hand on the forehead, the other cupping the occipital area at the back of the head if our person is experiencing distress. It really works. Sometimes, pain leaves, and stressors are diminished.

I found slowing down good for me and Gary. I may have felt hurried, but that unsettled him. I noticed my breath and moved slowly. He was also startled if I came from the side. I didn't understand why he jumped. People with dementia do not have clear peripheral vision. It is worth having this information.

Gary looked to see what was coming towards him from me and whether I approved. This may have been because I had growled a bit. I tried to have an open smiling face when I approached him, which is not always possible during a growl. I breathed into my heart, knowing I loved him. Compassion is essential.

I have learned not to argue. I generally agreed, even if I didn't know what he was saying. I resisted correcting him, I reminisced rather than taxing his memory, which dying brain cells do not support. This would have worked if the situation was not dangerous when a direct 'stop' or 'no' was needed. Learning has brought humility and self-forgiveness, as I have at times done all the recommended don'ts. An open heart to myself continued to be essential rather than guilt and blame.

At meals, Gary and I have always blessed the food. It settled him at the beginning of a meal. I lit a candle and dedicated it to those who are suffering. We said,

> May all beings have happiness, and the causes of happiness,
>
> May they be free from suffering and the causes of suffering,
>
> May they experience joy and the causes of joy,
>
> May they live in great equanimity, free from attachment and aversion.

Gary would often say random, kind words to support people in need, whatever came to his mind. There were times too, when his agitation took over, and he ate his food like a restless infant.

Caregiving with love invites so much more than a fondness for our person. The elements of true love can be summed up by the Buddhist teachings on the Four Immeasurable Minds:

Maitri, loving kindness or the desire to offer happiness.

Karuna, compassion or the desire to remove suffering from others.

Mudita, joy, or the desire to bring joy to others and allow their happiness to bring you joy.

Upeksha, equanimity or the desire to accept anything and not discriminate.

If we can train our minds to come from open-heartedness, happiness, compassion, or joy and to be willing to sit in the middle of what is happening in the moment without wishing it to be different, then we will be offering true love. In the mindset of these elements, we are living in the most beautiful, joyous, peaceful realm in the universe. We can aspire to this and notice our contractions even in the middle of despair. Contemplating the Four Immeasurable Minds can bring everything back into perspective.

Dementia can take memories of the past and those being made in the present, but it cannot take love. Love is energy. Keep touching with love in whatever way is possible. During times of Gary's irritation, I could touch from a distance, sending energy. I did tonglen, drawing the irritation from him and sending back love and my wish for him to be soothed. I tried to use my voice in a tender and loving way. Playing music to communicate worked at times. After all, research shows that even people in a coma hear at some level.

We are human and need to hear we are loved, which is often not possible through dementia responses, but if we know the love is there, maybe we need to listen differently. I relied on my memories of us together, trusting the enduring quality of love. Nature helped. Silence and meditation always help as we are not really doing this alone. Our ancestors come if we are open. Wanting things to be different gets in the way of Love.

Supporting a loved one through dementia is an act of selfless service, but our connection to our own needs cannot be neglected. When our glass is empty, we have nothing to give. Self-care is essential, even if we get it through self-soothing, painting, writing, music or remembering. We cannot want it from our loved ones in the way we have in the past. That expectation will lead to us suffering.

The visceral feeling when I was tired and Gary demanding: my body felt full right from my feet to the top of my head. There was very little brain space left to take in another need. If I tried to take in his need, it led to a nervous system reaction protecting me from annihilation (that is what it felt like). I acted in a callous and hurtful way, essentially attacking my enemy. I would go into a room, drink water, call a friend or nurse line to regulate myself to regain perspective. Dementia was at work, and self-care was my only way through.

Caregiving is spiritually challenging as we must put ourselves aside. The human spirit does not have dementia, the cells are dying. Gary was so much more than his brain cells. I could love his spirit easily, and he felt that love.

DEMENTIA AND OUR LOVE

12
GRIEF – SO MANY LOSSES

Dementia, Alzheimer's, and other life-limiting diseases are infused with loss. Life will never be the same again. I found myself angry, and when I *felt* into it, I found the hurt, sadness, and grief. The deeper the love or investment in the relationship, the deeper the grief.

In our Buddhist teachings, impermanence is front and center. We are all going to die, and nothing is permanent. Easy to say, but not easy to live. Knowing this, we are encouraged to love deeply all the time and make the most of our time here.

The initial loss with dementia was no longer being able to depend on our health. Very early on, Gary's walking became more of a shuffle, no more hikes, no traveling. The prognosis was grim, with no timeline. The cells would keep dying. He would forget memories, abilities, family members, and me.

Gary's losses were endless, and at first, he could look each one in the eye. The losses continued, and he wasn't aware of what was going on. With each loss, I assumed more responsibility, and he begrudged that. Anger is often present in helplessness. It covers the hurt so that we feel a little stronger. It is hard to grieve someone who is still here, but the feelings are all part of the process.

Tears came to my eyes often, noticing his frustration, feeling my exhaustion. I cried for myself and for Gary. Writing about our life opened my heart, and more tears came. Our love reminded me of impending loss. It is what they call anticipatory grief. Doctors said his brain would not be able to manage organs at some stage. I asked what we could anticipate. He could choke, get pneumonia, it was hard to say. He was deteriorating quite quickly in terms of cognitive function and mobility but was very much alive.

This grief does not allow us to mourn. We are too busy dealing with our person's life and needs. The end hovers like the shadow of a large dark boulder on the edge of a cliff, waiting precariously for conditions to change and gravity to take her reward.

Often, we will be told that dementia has changed someone, that the person is not there anymore. I have heard healthcare staff suggesting to family members," You must let go. You are just imagining what you want to believe". We do experience our loved ones differently. We feel their spirit. It may be a smile, a touch, a gesture, or a response to someone or something. The song of their life is not over, and like a beautiful flower, it needs watering.

Grief happens in the present, in the body, as we give space for our loved ones to make their journey toward the next stage. I already missed Gary and the fun and meaningful experiences we have had together, but I didn't spend much time mourning. That would come when Gary was gone. Who knows, maybe I would go first, and then I would have wasted this time of my living until the very end. Life is a mystery.

For grief to be healing, she must feel a relaxed container, the body, that allows her to spill tears, when necessary, without apology. These tears are medicine, both in the chemicals they release and in the movement of the heaviness of grief. In modern society, there is little time set aside for this ritual, and the tears are often held back like a dammed river, which overflows when it is full. Sometimes grief is equated with depression, as if it is something to be avoided, as 'it' makes us feel bad. Doctors will sometimes prescribe medications like anti-depressants to subdue our feelings and help us contain our grief.

The good news is that grief, when allowed, is full of love, as it opens our hearts to our vulnerable selves, which is more necessary than we can imagine. In vulnerability is enormous strength and resilience. There is risk too, but nothing other than our fear of what others may think or that we may have no reason to go on. Our ability to be real or authentic is dependent on some degree of vulnerability, so it is worth the risk.

An elder told her grandchild, who was grieving, "My child, go to the river and find a path alongside her banks. Face the way the river is going and walk with her. Give her your grief, your tears. She will gladly take them to the sea, to water's great home. When you need to leave the river, walk away, not back along the river, as it is not necessary to grieve the same grief over again. Each time it is new, and we let go. The river is our mother, she will be with us. We are never alone."

Grief and letting go ultimately take a different journey when persons with dementia enter the last stage. It is different for everyone. Gary had a healthy body, his only medication being for his thyroid. Over almost four years, he lost body and mind function. Doctors said he was deteriorating fast. He shuffled and refused for a long time to use a walker or wheelchair. He wanted to be seen to be independent. In what his gerontologist calls the end stage, Gary was literally fighting for his life. Major loss of brain function will eventually undermine a healthy body.

Any effort I made to make suggestions at this stage or my actions to make him comfortable were vehemently rejected. He was suspicious of my motivation, and he fought me with strong pulling away or forcing his way, fortunately without harming me.

Under normal circumstances, I would have considered it personally and emotionally abusive. He was hallucinating, thinking people were in the apartment. If the television was on, his perception was that the characters were in the room. It was confusing for him. The health workers visiting to give him a shower or for my respite became the enemy when they first arrived in the apartment. Most were able to pacify him during the visit.

He was king of the roost while I slept at night. In the morning, his clothing was scattered in various rooms. He was often wearing three socks on one foot, the other bare. His fixation was the bathroom, where creams and toothpaste were ingredients for his experiments. One night, I awoke to use the bathroom only to find him cleaning the toilet with a toothbrush. He used up a large spray bottle of environmentally sensitive bathroom cleaner.

One morning, his pull-ups were pulled apart inside the toilet bowl. I didn't realize how they were manufactured until I saw large fragments swelling like jellyfish. I salvaged this before it blocked the sewerage system in our building. The toilet brush was lathered in cream or toothpaste, maybe both, as an agent for cleaning no doubt.

It was winter, snowing and icy, so walking outside wasn't possible. Gary would look out, wanting to go somewhere by himself, angry that I seemed to make all the decisions. I would have hated being inside all the time, but safety was a concern. I would encourage him to wander inside, but no one was around, so it didn't serve his needs. His visits to the respite facility gave far more stimulation.

He was eventually assessed as number one on the *Intolerable Risk* list. I had to be patient while we waited for a bed. He would sometimes go back to sleep after his nightly adventures and wake up peacefully. I would feel able to care for him, and then agitation would unexpectedly rise, and a sleepless night would ensue, even with medication. His anger and violence against objects or his own body were disturbing.

Gary's grief during this stage was seldom tears. It came out in the form of anger and frustration, sometimes fear. He feared that nothing he did was right. It was not a time of vulnerability for Gary. He needed the strength of his masculinity. I say that not as a sexist comment, but it was mostly seen in front of men. My impression was he feared being seen as soft in front of his friends. This was interesting to observe, as Gary always had inner strength and was gentle and peaceful in his persona.

This stage can be difficult for caregivers. I accepted it as the last stage, one of many. The alternative was the hospital, where beds for people who are ill are at a premium. I felt impressed at Gary's strength of resistance, although it tired me, and I would go into my room for respite. The nights were cold, I would tuck his blankets around him, and he would throw them off. I would go to bed and let things unfold. In the morning, he would have a blanket wrapped around his head and torso, and his legs would be cold, but he wasn't in any danger. My motto was, "Do your best, then let go."

The tears, when they came, were naturally rising and brief. I let them be, but I, too, was in survival mode, so vulnerability could wait. I tried to stay soft-spoken and kind. I had to be more forceful when he was insisting on putting a sweater on feet-first as pants, and he may have fallen. His self-harm behavior was scary. He tried to shave his arm hair with a razor blade. He came through to my room with one arm red with blood running down in rivulets. He cut his hair and part of his beard. He would hit his head vigorously, sometimes against the wall. I stopped him at these times, sometimes forcefully, sometimes with care and kindness. I reported the incidents to his doctor. It was hard to watch, and I wanted to know how to support him.

The doctor called me and gave me suggestions for medication regimes, which I implemented as best I could. I tried behavioral interventions more often, particularly trying to help him calm down. He would follow me around and make a noise if I was busy. It was annoying, but I would walk from room to room. Thank goodness for cell phones. Friends got used to me speaking on the phone while driving or out walking.

I knew this would not last forever, and I was likely to really miss him when he was gone. I didn't want to regret his physical presence in my life. I would not remember him this way. This was dementia speaking and acting out. The writing helped. Each evening, I would read what I had written and remember him and our love before I went to sleep.

DEMENTIA AND OUR LOVE

13
CAREGIVING AS SPIRITUAL GROWTH

Is it sometimes difficult to love the person you are caregiving?

Let's face it, life is not perfect. Relationships are impacted by unhappiness and hard times. Sometimes, generational conditioning with a lack of communication or anger and violence is operating. These same family members also get old and need caregivers. I don't advocate martyrdom or being abused. In fact, this behavior can happen even in once-loving relationships.

Our self-care is crucial, particularly if we are in a difficult situation. This must continue during our visits or in the presence of the person. Breathe in and out smoothly and evenly. Focus your attention on your breath. Feel your feet on the floor or in your footwear. Stay grounded. Appreciate that you are being of benefit. Don't take their behavior personally (say to yourself, this is not about me). If they are hurtful verbally or physically, get additional help, you need to feel safe.

Khandro Rinpoche, a great Buddhist teacher, wrote in Shambhala Sun 13, 41 *Quintessence of compassion* in 2005, "Compassion is not about kindness. Compassion is about awareness, but one may not necessarily be free from ego-grasping. Genuine compassion is egoless. It arises as the ability to go beyond the self. It requires that we transcend the self." We matter too, but in our helping, we see ourselves and the person who is suffering in the same way without personally identifying with it. When helping, we cultivate the mind that wishes all that is good for our person. When they are reacting, they are just reacting. It is not personal, just an expression of their state of mind caused by their disease or suffering.

It is likely we won't be appreciated by people in this state of unhappiness, so don't expect it. Appreciate yourself. Practice self-compassion. Watch your mind, it may be filled with unpleasant memories of this person that are not conducive to your caring. Don't feed these thoughts, just attend to your breath. It is empowering to be free of reactivity. It is a spiritual quality that is worth cultivating. There are stories of people with some angry communication, settling down and changing when they don't get the reactions they have provoked.

Another strategy is to reflect on your relationship with the person you are supporting. Can you find times of tenderness and peace? Were they kind or generous to others at any point? Can we find some compassion for their lives? Being quiet during tasks or humming gently may soothe us, them too. Predictability can help, like checking in at the same time each day and keeping routines. Redirecting the person can be useful, quietly continuing the task and giving directions one at a time. What is it they like? What are their memories, photos, and music?

One reason I refer to caregiving as a practice capable of generating spiritual growth is because it is about focusing on meeting the needs of someone else, not us. I find that the needs of dementia and other conditions are all-consuming for the patient. They become self-absorbed and not aware of other's needs. Gary and I had equal roles in our life together. There was no expectation that I would do anything I did not choose to do in service to him. We were kind and considerate of one another, grateful and appreciative. This was no longer my experience of him, and I changed my expectations.

My ego wanted him to be appreciative and realize what was being done for him. This only caused disappointment. Dementia is in charge, and with brain cells dying, compassion is the only alternative. Caregiving is unconditional, bearing in mind we are still human. It really can, at times, be a state of grace.

Spiritual growth generally comes through times of difficulty. We often need to call on a deeper strength to get through the day. I reflect on the last three or four years and, how much I have learned, how much I have increased my capacity to love. I feel stronger and less self-centered. It does remind me of my time being a mother of young children. Their needs always had to come first. It was exhausting, but somehow, I managed to do my best (not always their best). Parents are doing this all around us.

I remember thinking at the beginning stages of dementia, "I was a mother of three young children. I have done my share!" It does feel remarkably similar sometimes. At one point, Gary was breaking his sandwich into pieces and offering some to me. It reminded me of an eighteen-month-old child in her highchair.

I also think about my privilege, having shelter, food, and enough cash to get by. Complaining doesn't seem relevant. Our home care support grew from two hours a week to nine hours, and we had a couple of doctors, nurses, and various people to help us, with the possibility of long-term care eventually. My connection with South Africa, Zimbabwe, Nepal, and India reminds me how caregivers, mostly women, step up to help others all the time with no compensation.

I remember the HIV and AIDs crisis particularly. I worked with caregivers who cared for the sick without pay. The groups I was asked to facilitate were to give them a chance to rest and recharge before they continued their generous service. They would tell me about arriving at an AIDs patient's house to ensure they took their ARV medication, which had to be taken with food. They said, "Well, at most homes, there was no food." I would ask them how they handled that. "We go back to our house and get whatever small piece of bread and return to our patient with it," they replied.

My suggestion to caregivers is to remember love is not just about our relationships. It is about love in all its many forms. In Southern Africa during the AIDs pandemic, I experienced deep love. My friend Aurelia, in South Africa runs a day-care program (with other women) for two hundred children every day, teaching and feeding them with minimal resources. Now, that is unconditional love.

Caregiver groups can be helpful, in person or online. I can only manage online these days, and I was invited to facilitate a group for hospice. We learned from one another and grew with one another. We shared small tips along the way, each of us experimenting and keeping our love alive. We would get through this, maybe thrive. I believe that love will sustain us in the end. Know that we caregivers are doing this in solidarity with one another. We are not alone.

It was a cold, rainy morning in December. I woke up at 6 am in the room next door to Gary. And reflected on the previous day. It started well with a gentle walk outside in the sun. Gary had two envelopes, one for Seva Canada, a cheque inside for eye care for children, and the other a cheque for the local food bank. He had a job, a generosity practice, and he was happy. We very slowly headed down the street to the mailbox. I helped, and he placed the Seva envelope safely in the slot.

We walked on one block and slowly made our way up the ramp to the food bank. His legs were beginning to falter. Gary handed a young employee the envelope. I asked if we could sit for a short while. An older woman whom I see in the garden, when she is walking, leered into my face, "So you have found yourself a boyfriend." People snickered. They knew her. I smiled and nodded. Gary drank coffee, and we chatted with the fellow across the table. He told us the lunch was good.

It was time for us to head home and we made our way down to the street and walked the half-block home, headed upstairs in the elevator, and arrived in our apartment. It was time for our lunch, and I placed humus, avocado and olives out for Gary. I made his sandwich, and we ate together. He took his sandwich apart in small pieces, I strategically moved his mat closer to catch the food, he moved it away. Oh well!

Gary insisted on helping to clean his plate, and I left the kitchen in his hands, there was a basin of water ready. After a few minutes, he walked to where I was sitting in the living room and showed me the olive container empty and clean. I asked, "Where are the olives?" He couldn't tell me. I felt agitated as the container had in it almost $10 worth of dried olives at lunch. I looked inside the compost, no olives, the refrigerator, no olives. I noticed the water in the basin had a dark blackish hue. There they were dumped in the dirty water, but their container was clean, and Gary was happy. I felt the need to explain solemnly what he had done. He looked confused. He was only trying to help.

I walked away tired, not wanting his company for a while. He took off his sweater for the fifth time that day, tugging at the zipper which I had sewn shut at the bottom as it was broken. I told him it must come over his head. He got lost in the arm holes, and I helped. A little later, he was cold and asked for a jacket, and so it went. We made it through the afternoon watching one of the many stories of Bob Dylan while I sat with my laptop, editing.

Gary paced, changing clothes, restlessness had started early. I gave him his medication and figured out a simple evening meal, tacos. He seemed to like the idea and hovered very close to me as I navigated our small kitchen, being mindful of hot pans and oven. The tacos had beans, cheese, avocado and salsa with a salad on the side. I joined him at the table, and the chess game began with the mat being the chess piece. Apparently, this meal was for hands, and the beans squished easily through his fingers. My housekeeping mind was on the potential mess. He reached out to me, offering a piece of his soft, unrecognizable taco. I declined and finished my salad with very little appetite left. We made it through another day.

Gary was ready to sleep at 6.30 pm. My task was to keep him awake as long as possible so that he wouldn't spend his nights wandering through the apartment while I slept. I sighed with relief as I tucked his blankets around him at 7.45 pm and kissed him. I returned to my chair to read for a while. The night game was on: Gary appeared with a big smile. I felt tired and annoyed and chose not to communicate. He was restless, and I eventually walked him back to bed, the same ritual as before. I switched off the lights and closed my door. He came to visit one more time. I told him to go away. I felt exhausted, muttering, "This is getting to be too much!"

Dementia And Our Love

I meditated before going to sleep as it really did help and awoke at 6 am. I thought about my writing on a heart-felt approach to caregiving and how unloving I had been at the end of the day before. It was time to reconnect. I made my way into Gary's room and snuggled under the covers next to him. His body felt warm and inviting, his love right there welcoming me towards him. He seemed so happy I was there. My eyes were weeping, tears running down my face. He held me as if to say," Here we are, I haven't gone anywhere." I could feel it too. His energy was still there. His spirit was present.

Love is a vibration, a pulse, if we are open and not grasping. I am grateful for the moments when I can feel it. The story-making about love requires cognition which dementia takes at every turn. I find the feeling of love more reliable than the story. It is primitive and silently present when we are attentive to it. When I am tired, I am not as attentive, just as Gary was not attentive to love when he was restless. The early morning, if we had slept, provided the conditions to experience love, so I was more often taking this time to be with him. I am aware of Gary's poem to me from La Penita,

I want to make love with you,

Not with our sexual organs,

But breathing Ishq

Into each other's mouth.

You know Ishq, the love nectar of the gods,

The creator of sand and ocean,

The vulture, you, and me.

This is the love he was talking about. I could feel it, and it felt precious and profound.

I traveled to my daughters and grandchildren for two weeks over Christmas in 2023, and Gary spent time in respite. It was the longest time apart in several years. He was naturally disoriented when I brought him home. We had reached a new level as he was incontinent and his communication indecipherable. I sighed as I tried to understand him or have him understand me. I quickly became tired and irritable as I was faced with the reality of the care needed. He visited me three times that night and was very busy around the house taking things apart, eating, changing clothes, and eventually going to bed exhausted.

The next day, after a long sleep-in, it was as if nothing had happened. In terms of spiritual teachings, dementia provides great growth opportunities and is life-giving for me. Again, it reminded me that we caregivers must not take anything personally and yet keep our hearts open. I reflect on how little I have learned in this regard and how much I need to practice this art. The beauty of dementia is the lack of memory, so I could start again at any time. Gary didn't hold a grudge. He didn't blame but was ready for the next moment.

My meditation teacher, Lama Tara, held a practice session on zoom for an hour. I invited Gary to be in the room. He had been a regular meditator for forty years. He lay on my bed; I sat in a chair facing the screen. It was exactly what I needed. He seemed asleep, but as soon as we finished after an hour, he sat up and looked deeply into my eyes. He was totally present. He said, "This was good." I decided to include him in my daily meditation practice in the same way, with no expectation of it being 'good' for him the next time.

Caregiving is the greatest teacher of impermanence or change as the body and mind of our loved ones move toward the end of their lives. If I stayed present and noticed myself with tenderness breathing in and out, I noticed my feet on the ground. I felt supported.

I might say courtesy of Thich Nhat Hanh

> I am alive,
>
> I am well,
>
> In the here and the now.
>
> No coming, nor going,
>
> In the ultimate I dwell.

I would feel more at home in myself, and if I was attentive, I might, for a short time appreciate that I was the exhausted caregiver, I was the joyful nature explorer, I was the breath.

Dementia and Our Love

Thich Nhat Hanh writes,

> Please call me by my true names
> so I can hear all my cries and laughter at once,
> so I can see that my joy and pain are one.
> Please call me by my true names,
> so I can wake up
> and the door of my heart
> can be left open,
> the door of compassion.

Self-compassion is a prerequisite for our compassion for others. When I embrace what I am experiencing as part of love, not separate from love, I am more likely to ride the waves of change without grasping or aversion. We are all connected to the river of Life. This is the love that gives back. It fills me up. I feel connected to life, and this connection serves me. I am more aware of what I am being called to do.

I was particularly tired and frustrated one day, and I walked out of our apartment, intent on taking a walk in the forest. As I was heading to the car, a voice in my head said, "Go and see Jim." I, for an instant, disagreed and set out to drive to the forest. The voice again said, "Go and see Jim in the hospital." Gary and I had visited him the day before, but I listened and drove to the hospital.

I arrived at Jim's room on the second floor, and the curtain was drawn around his bed. I waited to see if this was an appropriate time. I heard Jim speaking. He said to his wife, "Please contact Heather and Gary to come and see me." I spoke up. I had appeared as if out of nowhere, just as he had made the request. His wife left to do errands.

Jim was very close to death. He needed to say certain things to me. We spoke of life and his imminent death. He had questions. I didn't have answers but could share the experiences of others who had gone before. He said he felt reassured and ready.

That night, I returned with Gary to say goodbye. They were dear friends. He was in severe pain. He held Gary's hand. I stood next to him, breathing in his pain and sending love, my hand on his heart. He told Gary to appreciate me as he appreciated his wife. He said how lucky he and Gary were to have us in their lives. Jim died the following day, his wife and nephew at his side.

True love is imbued with respect and gratitude for the common purpose, the joys and growth that come out of difficulties. I have gratitude for this opportunity for us to serve one another, for in doing this, we serve ourselves and all sentient beings.

The restlessness, delusion, agitation, and anger became worse in mid-January 2024. I tried my best speaking softly, wrapping his cut arm so he wouldn't cause infection, discouraging self-harm, and dealing with all the health support people. Gary was very unhappy. I realized that I had reached the wall. He seemed in an allergic response. I mentioned it to the doctor and Gary vehemently shook his head. "It is about my love for you," he said. I could do nothing for him. I was so weary.

I made his dinner, and he banged on everything he touched. I wanted to close my door, and it struck me that this was the last time we would be together in our home. The tears came. There was no coming back from this. I went into his room, where he was stretched out on the bed. He was listening to an Indigenous program. Gary was speaking of a simple death. I asked about it, but he was talking to himself. I told him how much I loved him. He dosed off. This time is precious, I thought.

The phone call came from the social worker at a care home close to where we lived. There were many details, what to bring, what to expect. We were given two days. I decided to use the word respite as he knew it from previous respite visits. My sadness filled my chest like an object being inflated, getting tighter and tighter. I breathed, and it filled my throat, but had nowhere else to go. I was unable to say goodbye to people who called.

Kirstie offered to accompany us. At first, I declined but was encouraged to take her loving offer. This was bigger than the delivery of Gary to respite. The practical would take precedence allowing the grief short bursts until he was settled. I had a good support system.

So, this was it. Gary would be leaving home permanently, and I could visit whenever I liked. I wondered what this would be like. The time together was precious and short. Two days later, we set off with a suitcase, picture collage of family and friends, radio, and walker. Kirstie lovingly accompanied me as we entered the final stage of our journey, living together in love.

The first two weeks were naturally difficult for Gary as he adjusted to those around him. I visited each day for a couple of hours. I realized I had entered a liminal space, being both independent and alone at home and part of the care facility. I attended to my personal life by walking, swimming laps at the pool, and even going to the gym to ride a bicycle. I needed to be in my body.

I still wrote somewhat and prepared the book for publication as I wanted to share it with Gary. Reading our story helped me. The tears came at will just like air bubbles trapped underwater and then released into the air. I reorganized some of the disarray from the past few years and made myself comfortable.

My visits with Gary became fascinating as my first impression was of the disengagement of the residents. I noticed their awareness of one another and the environment. They had individual communication systems. What I had initially seen as odd behavior without purpose, I realized had a function. One time, watching Gary, I saw his eyes crinkle at the corners, smiling, as he sat back and watched an interaction. The person making the sounds was being quite deliberate, and he seemed to be appreciating her intent and watching for results. There was humor.

The slow pace meant I had to slow down and be quiet. The impassive faces during the first week as I arrived became friendly. I was greeted in small ways and felt accepted into the community. I reflected on how I have entered new situations as a confident, white, educated, middle class woman. Humility is a difficult practice for settlers. In South Africa and Zimbabwe, I had to be aware of myself entering quietly, without dominance, open to learning, always open to learning, waiting to be invited in.

This is also my experience in Quw'utsun territory, where I live here in Duncan. I know I have privilege, but healing and reconciliation require humility. I am fortunate to have some of this awareness and practice as I enter the dementia community. I have so much to learn. Siyafunda in isixhosa, a prominent South African language, means we are learning. I hope this continues and that I can continue to participate with kindness.

I was told that with Gary in care, I could return to being his spouse. This is true. I am not an exhausted caregiver. I am taking my time resuming my life quietly and often alone as I listen to my inner knowing of what is needed in each moment. I stay present as dementia makes no promises.

DEMENTIA AND OUR LOVE

14
Gratitude And Learning

The work of the mature person is to carry grief in one hand and gratitude in the other and to be stretched large by them. How much sorrow can I hold? That's how much gratitude I can give. If I carry only grief, I'll bend toward cynicism and despair. If I only have gratitude, I'll become saccharine and won't develop much compassion for other people's suffering. Grief keeps the heart fluid and soft, which makes compassion possible.

Francis Weller, *The Wild Edge of Sorrow*

This journey with Gary and dementia required me to carry a bag in each hand to stay balanced. Sometimes, the bag of showing up and responding to the constant demands was so heavy it almost dragged on the ground. This is when I closed my bedroom door and focused on the beautiful life I have chosen or walked in the forest, grateful to be alive. Genuine gratitude is in this bag.

Meditation sharpens the clarity of the mind, resulting in awareness of what is happening in each moment. I am grateful beyond measure for this practice. The balance between commitment to others and to self allows a greater capacity for loving and serving. It opens the heart.

I am also grateful for the moments when we connected, the moments when we laughed and had fun, the moments when we remembered who we really are. Dementia antics can be really funny at times. We can experience challenging times and then wake up the next day ready to start again with good feelings for one another. We knew we were much more than an illness. I will remember our life together. I have enjoyed sharing.

Dementia And Our Love

Sitting together

Playing music

GRATITUDE AND LEARNING

Being a family

Dementia And Our Love

Beloved Gary,

Thank you for sharing the last twenty-six years with me. We jumped in and lived truthfully. We loved until the end, even if dementia tried to have her way. I can't pretend it was easy the last three years, but we recognized impermanence and started again with good hearts every day. I was the one making many decisions, and you have always valued your independence. I have been in awe of your resistance, not willing to give up, and it has challenged me. You are strong and committed. I love that about you.

Probably my greatest practice has been not taking things personally. Some days, it was so clearly dementia on a rant. Other days, the anger coming at me felt bruising. I needed a little time to be fully open-hearted again. Even after some harsh words, you managed to let me know you loved me and checked that I loved you. I do and always will. It is rare to live with another human with such transparency.

I am grateful beyond words for the Buddha dharma with teachings we could trust, one of which is to be grateful for the difficulties that come our way. They are indeed our teachers. If we consciously employ the teachings to get through in a good way, it is possible to be of benefit to one another and all beings.

We have had fun, we have laughed and cried together. At times, we lived with grace and freedom on very little. We connected with ourselves, one another, and so many extraordinary beings. Buddhism has taught us about death and given practices for this transition.

In your new situation, I will continue to visit regularly and love you just as much. I will also be your wife without the constant instructions. I will share our story and trust it will be of benefit.

Thank you for who you are and who I am because of you.

I will always remember us this way.

My love always

Heather

"There is nothing that can replace the absence of someone dear to us, and one should not even attempt to do so. One must simply hold out and endure it. At first, that sounds very hard, but at the same time, it is also a great comfort. For to the extent, the emptiness truly remains unfilled, one remains connected to the other person through it. It is wrong to say that God fills the emptiness. God in no way fills it, but much more leaves it precisely unfilled and thus helps us preserve - even in pain - the authentic relationship. Furthermore, the more beautiful and full the remembrances, the more difficult the separation, but gratitude transforms the torment of memory into silent joy. One bears what was lovely in the past, not as a thorn but as a precious gift deep within, a hidden treasure of which one can always be certain.

Dietrich Bonhoeffer

On a lighter note, this is for Gary. He was traveling across the border into Canada from the United States in the seventies. He and his friends were always nervous, hoping not to be apprehended for anything. He stepped up to the immigration officer, who looked at his passport and then his face. He paused, and Gary held his breath. The officer said, "How come they call you Lips?" Gary had no idea what he was talking about. The officer grinned, and Gary relaxed. "They sometimes call me Bean but not Lips," he replied with a smile.

Today, I realized the insight of that immigration officer, little did he know. Gary transfers his love for me through his lips even now. He met me today when I visited Sunridge, our lips connected, and I could feel the fullness of his love. In that moment, there was no time, no dementia and no separation, just pure love. Then he wandered back content to his room and fell asleep.

Gratitude And Learning

DEMENTIA AND OUR LOVE

Acknowledgements and Gratitude

I am forever grateful to my parents, who taught me that life is a spiritual journey being lived in physical form, not the other way around. I appreciate my friend Shelah, who introduced me to Buddhist teachings. Thank you to all my beautiful, compassionate teachers. To the late Kristeen Verge, my dear friend who instigated the trip to Mexico.

To my first husband Stuart, who chose me to accompany him through his journey with terminal brain cancer in South Africa when I was twenty-five and twenty-six. We did it without medication, just freshly juiced grapes and herbs. I had no experience other than a belief in what might be possible. There was no hospice to help support me as a caregiver. Stuart and I went day-to-day supported by a natural medicine practitioner. I learned so much about life, death, and grieving that ultimately led me into psychotherapeutic work with living and dying. Once I discovered the hospice movement, I developed a deep connection to the work of hospice training and supporting people with death and dying.

To hospice staff, volunteers, and caregivers everywhere. You have taught me so much with your loving presence, generosity, and willingness to accompany people at the end of life (no matter how long it takes). To my caregiving group at Cowichan Valley Hospice and Cowichan Caregivers, Dr Hargrove and Chris Parry RN, Dr Ismail, the home care team, and Sunridge Place, thank you from the bottom of my heart.

To my children Kirstie, Wendy and Robyn, and grandchildren Emilie, Milo, Charley, Zoey, and Finley, who have supported us and missed out on my support during the last four years. To Jenny, always loving and here for us on behalf of the sibs. Big hugs and kisses. Thank you, Nancie, for your love and support. To CM, Daniel, Jim and Rick, such supportive friends.

To South African women who are strong and loving caregivers in situations of great need. Their hearts, wisdom, and generosity guide me. Their friendship brought me home to myself with humility.

Thank you to the Federation of BC Writers, Matt Rudnitsky of Punchy Books, and Lady Gaga for her inspirational song, *Always Remember Us This Way*. Jenny Ferris, Monica Mueller, Peter Fox, Pam Webster, and my community of readers of the introduction, who encouraged me to publish. A very warm thanks to Teepa Snow for your heart-felt and skillful knowledge and teaching about dementia and your kindness in writing the foreword.

To my beloved, Gary, who has been an extraordinary partner in this life, and who has taught me through his life (including dementia), what meditation and service is truly about. We do this together in love.

REFERENCES

Bonhoeffer, Dietrich (1953). Letters and Papers from Prison.
United Kingdom: SCM

Chodron, Pema (2000). *When Things Fall Apart.*
Boulder Co: Shambhala Publications.

Ferris, Charles (1997). Columba Speaks p.115.
Victoria BC: Melville Publications.

Gibran, Kahlil (1923). The Prophet
London: Heinemann.

Hanh, Thich Nhat (1993). Please Call Me By My True Names.
Berkeley CA: Parallax Press.

Khandro Rinpoche (2005). Quintessence of compassion Khandro Rinpoche, Shambhala Sun magazine 13, 41 (now known as Lion's Roar)

Snow, Teepa (2021). Understanding The Changing Brain
Positive Approach

Weller, Francis (2015). The Wild Edge of Sorrow
Berkeley CA: North Atlantic Books

Dementia And Our Love

Further Information

For more information about Teepa Snow and her Positive Approach to Care®, please visit www.teepasnow.com

Publications by Heather Ferris: www.heatherjferris.com

Psoriasis Healing from the Inside Out (1995) Amazon.com

Author: Heather Ferris

> This book encourages a different view of healing, one in which we have more control of the outcome, and the psoriasis diminishes as well. This is Heather's own story.

Someone I Love Died (2011) Amazon.com

Author Heather Ferris

> A book written for young people who have lost a significant person through death. It is set in South Africa during the HIV and AIDs crisis and follows stories of teens in a support group and their responses to their loss and healing. It includes at-the-back tips for parents who would like to support their teens.

Mindfulness, Awakening to A Meaningful Life (2011) Amazon.com

A pocketbook reminding us of key life principles and practices, including mindfulness meditation.

Publications by Charles Ferris: (contact Heather heatherferris46@gmail.com)

Twelve Dimensions, a story of life after death

Columba Speaks, Wisdom for the 21st century

The Ghost of Lylalee, Past lives and their affect on the present life

Angels of Mercy, A dream of peace in Ireland

A Small Gift, Healings experienced by Charles Ferris

Publication by I. Henriette Ferris:

Waking to the Light (2011) Amazon.com

The story of Inez Henriette Ferris's awakening, including the Ferris family's Faith Trip.

E-mail: heatherferris46@gmail.com

PLEASE CONSIDER SUPPORTING AND/OR LEARNING FROM:

SEVA Canada www.seva.ca Restoring sight in low- and middle-income countries

Rokpa International www.rokpa.org Humanitarian aid to vulnerable people around the world

Love and Care Day Centre, Masiphumelele South Africa www.heatherjferris.com

The Lama Foundation www.lamafoundation.org A spiritual community embracing traditions, an educational facility and retreat center near Taos, New Mexico

About the Author

Heather Ferris is a compassionate psychotherapist in private practice, a trainer working with hospice volunteers and community grief. She is also a speaker, workshop presenter and a teacher of mindfulness meditation, providing 5-day silent retreats.

Heather has been a caregiver to her husband Gary, who has had dementia since 2020, first at home and now in a residential care setting. Heather and Gary spent 20 years working with caregivers and HIV and AIDs in Southern Africa as payback for leaving her country (South Africa) during apartheid. She is still very much involved with the Love and Care Day Centre in Masiphumulele, Cape Town. Gary Greenstein participated in the writing of this memoir by gifting his poetry and emails expressing his love.

DEMENTIA AND OUR LOVE

DEMENTIA AND OUR LOVE

Manufactured by Amazon.ca
Acheson, AB